CROSSING THE RIVER:
Essays in Honour of Margaret Laurence

CROSSING THE RIVER:

Essays in Honour of Margaret Laurence

Kristjana Gunnars, Editor

TURNSTONE PRESS

Turnstone Press gratefully acknowledges the assistance of the Manitoba Arts Council, the Manitoba Department of Culture, Heritage and Recreation, and the Canada Council.

Turnstone Press
607-100 Arthur Street
Winnipeg, Manitoba
R3B 1H3

The cover photo of Margaret Laurence, from the film *Speaking Our Peace*, is used by permission of The National Film Board of Canada.

Cover design: Ernie Reichert, Sleeping Tiger Artworks

This book was printed by Hignell Printing Limited for Turnstone Press.

Printed and bound in Canada

Canadian Cataloguing in Publication Data

Main entry under title:

Crossing the river

Includes bibliographical references.
ISBN 0-88801-128-8

1. Laurence, Margaret, 1926- 2. Authors, Canadian (English)—20th century—Biography.*
I. Laurence, Margaret, 1926- II. Gunnars, Kristjana, 1948-

PS8523.A86Z57 1988 C813'.54 C88-098098-2
PR9199.3.L385Z57 1988

Contents

Kristjana Gunnars

Preface

IT WAS A WINTER DAY in Winnipeg: the kind of day when all is stilled and seized in layers of ice. A casual lunch meeting with Dennis Cooley, on that otherwise ordinary day, brought up the topic of Margaret Laurence. Friends had written me some time earlier to say she was ill and had only a short time left to live. It was not something we were prepared to believe. Margaret Laurence seemed destined to be with us indefinitely. She and her work had burned themselves into our consciousness to such a degree that her departure seemed incomprehensible. We decided the rumour must be exaggerated. Nonetheless we were impressed by the limits of human mortality. I mention this occasion because it is important to this book: if we had not met that day, this collection might not have materialized as it did. My idea for some kind of *Festschrift* for Margaret Laurence had found sympathetic ears. We decided then and there to put all wheels into motion, to work quickly and have a book in her hands within a few months. We wanted her to see it. We thought we could do it.

It was somehow important to show our appreciation for what she had accomplished in her life. Margaret Laurence has been a founding mother of Canadian literature. She has given voice to the Manitoba prairie. She has raised the value of all sectors of society by showing the full humanity of the most neglected and forgotten among us. From her example we have learned the value of Canadian literature and culture; the importance of art to that culture; the necessity of honesty in a dangerous time in history; the truth of fiction and poetry. Perhaps her greatest gift has been the way in which she showed us the depths and passions of the place in which we were living: Manitoba, through her, had taken full part in the human drama. We no longer needed to look elsewhere. Our first idea was to make it a Manitoba *Festschrift*, with contributions from her fellow writers there. This idea was partly necessitated by the speed with which we had to work.

Some time later, after more meetings with Turnstone Press and the Manitoba Arts Council, as we were going ahead with our plans, news reached us that Margaret Laurence had passed away. Our dreams of giving her this book were gone, but new ideas came in their place. Since we had time, we could change the nature of the collection and do what I most wanted to do all along. This was to gather longer, considered, thoughtful and well-researched essays from across the country, and also from abroad if possible. Margaret Laurence's work has impacted on all parts of Canada, not only Manitoba. She has had an influence beyond the borders of Canada as well. She is read, admired and studied all over the world. Some of this reality, I felt, ought to be mirrored in a serious collection of essays that are meant to contribute to Laurence scholarship.

The resulting book contains 12 essays. Ten of these are investigations into various aspects of Laurence's work. The other two, the introductory and afterword essays, focus on Laurence the person and her life. The ten approaches to Laurence's writings offered here are quite different in emphasis and subject matter. However, they all treat her novels, short stories and non-fiction with the sense of importance as well as affection they deserve. Some views and arguments here will conflict: each author sets him or herself a topic of inquiry and works the argument through to the end, given the understanding the research reveals. The book is meant to be a forum for debate; a kind of panel to spark further debate elsewhere. Readers will find that most of the contributors make use of the same source material to some extent, for Laurence scholarship is still in its beginning stages and we have only a limited number of books on her work to consult. But it will probably be of interest to see the different ways these secondary sources are used.

Margaret Laurence writes about people who have not easily become either heroes or anti-heroes in our literature. These are people largely ignored for lack of interest: old women; single women in middle age; people on the fringes of society who do not fully participate in the system. She pushes us to see their full value as human beings and to participate in forms of anti-drama: concerns and events that are traditionally considered boring or trivial. She writes about the kind of people who do not ordinarily fascinate us, and she emphasizes our tendency to ignore or reject them by surrounding her main characters with people who react similarly. It is a mark of Laurence's genius that she can make whatever she focusses on interesting. She can change our perspective by showing what our environment, its people and places, is composed of in terms of human value. Her most significant gift may be the reminder her work issues in all its force that we are fools to create outcasts. That we are misguided to think ourselves better than anyone else; that ambition, wealth, power, status are things that entirely miss the point. True value is somewhere else, and her journey is a slow discovery of where that "somewhere else" is.

All of the contributors to this collection seem to be in accord with this point, and they all set out to show something of where Laurence places that critical and important value.

Constance Rooke reasserts the possibility, even the necessity, of passionate drama, with all the conflicts and tensions of high adventure, in the end of an old person's life. Using *The Stone Angel* as an example, she asks us to see the story of life's "winding down" as a genre, a *Vollendungsroman*, much as we have seen the story of "winding up" in the *Bildungsroman* and the creation of an artist in the *Künstlerroman*. As Tolstoy's "The Death of Ivan Ilych" shows, what happens at the edge of the grave may have the life's climax, or epiphany, in it: at no point can we leave a character behind and say his or her development and change is complete. As a genre, the novel of "old age" has its own characteristics and patterns, and this essay helps us to acquire ways of thinking about Laurence's concerns in fiction. In doing so, we find that the old woman—the figure so frequently bypassed, ignored, undermined, manipulated, in life as well as fiction—is in fact living life at its most intense.

For Paul Hjartarson, the value lies in a reshifting of the relation between myth and reality. He proposes that Laurence emphasizes the importance of myth—not necessarily *over* reality, but in equal status to it. In a person's search for identity, and especially for roots, the journey may not be geographical or genetic. Using *The Diviners* as his case study, he points out that Morag Gunn is both adopted and separated from the geographical roots of her ancestors. But she finds that neither of these facts matter: her roots have grown through the soil of myth. Her adoptive father, Christie, has generated myths of ancestry for her, with which she identifies. Through the myths, her true parentage is to be found in the *teller* of the stories that create her. Therefore the position of the story and the narrator of that story acquire central importance. Fiction transcends reality and becomes the most important part of our lives. Here we may see something of Laurence's purpose as a writer, and we find a connection between the business of writing and the story-telling of other societies she has experienced in Africa. The writer is the mythmaker, the shaman, the priest. On another level, what is significant about the observations of this essay has everything to do with "ethnic" communities in Canada: it is a mistake to think North American "ethnic" groups are carrying on with cultures of the old country. To the contrary, these groups have cultures all their own; myths of origin not necessarily shared by the old country.

Craig Tapping then informs us of the nature of Margaret Laurence's experience in Africa and how she came to identify Canada in colonial terms. Laurence made an effort to understand her Nigerian counterparts and the literature of the native speakers. A personal note is struck when the author of the essay, as a young instructor in eastern Nigeria, discovers that Margaret Laurence has been there before him and made her mark. He is led to reflect on the African origins of Laurence's fiction: what she owes to the Nigerian culture of story-telling and writing and how she redefines the Canadian experience in terms of what she learns abroad. This essay pushes us to see Canadian literature in the same way, and one of the outstanding comments made here is that we are still behind Nigeria in the incorporation of our own literature into the official educational system. Indeed, it *is* possible to graduate from a Canadian university in English "without having encountered any national literature." While saying all this, Craig Tapping brings Laurence's early work—her essays and Somali translations, often overshadowed by the later fiction—to our attention.

A further investigation into the art of story-telling, and its central importance in Laurence's fiction, is offered by David Williams. His essay on story within story assumes as a starting point what has been proposed in the preceding essays. If Constance Rooke alerts us to the nature of Laurence's quest for identity; Paul Hjartarson to the significance of myth to that quest; and Craig Tapping to the debt owed here to Somali oral culture, then David Williams takes on the story-teller's garb and allows narrative its full place. Only here it is the metafiction which also becomes fiction: the one who talks about story talking about story is only passing on a kind of orality inherent in the fiction itself. This essay makes us feel that the boundaries we have drawn between written and oral literature is artificial. The critic is inspired to creativity while engaged in reflection on sources and their sources. The joy of reading and writing emerges: the original author has become a shaman who sets worlds in motion. We recognize with the essay that we are all engaged in encountering, absorbing and passing on the many myths, sayings, puns, idioms, parables that are the business of literature and the ingredients of our reality.

But, lest we go too far with this world of the spirit, we are brought back to the hard edges of a reality we share and for which Laurence never ceased to have concerns. Keith Louise Fulton takes another look at the humanist tradition which has engendered the values we live by, and finds that it reflects insufficiently on the lives of the women who partake in it. The redefinitions inherent in Laurence's work are deeper than a centralizing of the marginalized and a focussing in on native Canadian orality and story—in opposition to a falsifying official European-based tradition. Laurence's work constitutes a restructuring of our philosophical foundations. The old assumptions on which our activities and opinions are based are crumbling. This essay reminds us of Laurence's sense of grief over the political nature of our conduct and the destructive power of international military arsenals. Language, rhetoric, have not been able to keep up with cold reality on this front: therefore we face "a crisis of the imagination." Feminism has pointed out that the factors contributing to this crisis involve the exclusion of the female perspective; therefore there is a denial of the full humanity that is meant to make up the humanist tradition. By making women speak, Laurence shows the inadequacy of our inherited ways of thinking.

However, there is nothing didactic about Laurence. Her fiction does not have an overt "message" and it does not lecture at us. Nor is there any sentimentality in the concerns and conflicts raised in her books. As pointed out in the introductory essay by Walter Swayze, there may appear to be a Christian "message" in Laurence's work, but that is not evident to many. Hans Hauge presents a way of reading her works as religious texts and shows that more is demanded of the reader than simply passive absorption. In this essay, we are reminded that literature is not what it *says*, but what it *does*. What effect it has on the reader. For this look at Laurence, Hans Hauge draws from the theories of the deconstructionists as well as from theology. It is our concept of Christian ideas that is faulty when we cannot see the religious value of novels such as *The Stone Angel*. It is not order and control and message that reveal the true bias of such a book: its theology is to be found in its disorder, apparent lack of control, and effect. If we can be moved to feel affection for Hagar, the work is accomplished.

The same note is struck by Aritha van Herk as regards feminist readings of Laurence. Focussing on *A Jest of God*, this essay argues against former thematic and mimetic readings and proposes an alternative way of understanding what the text is doing rather than saying. It is not of great consequence *what* Rachel says. What matters is *how*, and more importantly, *that* she says or speaks at all. We are asked to reinvest the spinster figure with all of the erotic and passionate intensity that comes with being human. Stereotypes are narrowing and Laurence has not given us characters that lend themselves to stereotyping. Something about them cries out to be heard in their full humanity. Aritha van Herk also sounds a note we find in David Williams' essay: creation creates creation. There is joy in reading, absorbing and writing again. There is joy in rereading. Metafiction of the kind given us by these two authors reminds us that literature, when it is deep and reverberating enough, as Laurence's is, need never lose its vitality and intensity for us.

Helen Buss, on the other hand, takes us back through all

the preceding essays to another beginning. Her article takes a look at possible relationships between Laurence's fiction and her life. Here she carries on with concerns raised by Craig Tapping and makes a similar claim for strong autobiographical undercurrents in all of Laurence's prose. Some aspects of autobiographical fiction are raised and the business of truth becomes, after all, significant. Not necessarily truth of fact, but truth of feeling and experience. Autobiographical and creative readings of Laurence may seem to be in opposition, but Paul Hjartarson's essay is there to show how they see-saw on an identical pivotal point. In her investigations of the autobiographical factor, Helen Buss provides a great deal of information on Laurence's life. What we learn about Laurence's African experiences and her shock over the realities of colonialism and women's lives she sees there, are especially significant. When we come to Diana Brydon's essay, the considerations posed by Helen Buss are of interest.

Taking a step back to acquire greater critical distance, Herbert Zirker brings into focus the function and position of the literary critic. It is well to ask what we do, as critics, and what lies behind the way we do it. The focal point of this essay is Laurence's story "The Loons," of *A Bird in the House*, and the author looks at the relationship between semantics and meaning or implied meaning. The assumption here is that Laurence does indeed have something to say, but she says it indirectly. The question is not so much what the story *does*, except in its use of the emotional milieu of words which affect us, but what it says in its semantic complexities. The native speaker of Manitoban English will presumably find reverberations in Laurence's language that outsiders do not see or feel. Those reverberations constitute undercurrents of reading which exist for those who understand them. But, as Aritha van Herk and David Williams show, the undercurrents may be picked up and sounded by a good critic, and as Diana Brydon shows, they may also be explained. But it is Herbert Zirker who makes us remember that there are fictions within fictions, sometimes invisible to the superficial reader.

Diana Brydon proposes a woman's reading of Laurence's works, and she focusses on the five main female characters of her major fiction. What strikes a woman about these works is not the politics of the marginalized or the history of the language used. The important business, instead, is the relationship between voice and silence. There is, as Constance Rooke shows, a search for identity. It may be, as Helen Buss claims, partly the author's own search for identity—and even, as Walter Swayze thinks, something she learned only while writing. But the function of the narrative is all-important: to find a voice for that which is so difficult to say becomes the primary quest. The image of the mirror is interesting: it has a history coming down to us from its prominence in Medieval times, when the image of the woman holding a mirror was focal. But that is only an image: it is a silent image which cannot sound any voice. And it is true that, in retrospect, Laurence's novels have an air of incredible and vast silence about them. Partly it is the setting—the Manitoba prairie and small town—and partly it is the inarticulate suppression the main characters have undergone. But in this silence there is a great deal of suffering, and speaking becomes a way of relieving that suffering. In the end, speaking is all: narrative is all.

So we have, in a way, gone full circle through some of the most important considerations of Laurence's works. To introduce us to all these questions, Walter Swayze has provided a full and powerful overview of Margaret Laurence the woman, the humanitarian, the political realist and the creative writer. Through this essay, written by a long-time friend and associate (now Professor Emeritus and Honorary Fellow of United College, the latter the distinction that Margaret Laurence received in 1966), we see Laurence as she was and acquire an understanding of why she has been so much loved, both as a person and as a writer. We are also given a perspective on the impact of her work in Canada and the nature of her origins. She has always had one focus of attention, above all others: people. In all their difficulty, pain, foolishness, Margaret Laurence's life work has been for and about people. Whether they suffer or are happy, whether they treat each other ill or well, were her concerns. This essay shows abundantly that if there is one word that will describe Margaret Laurence, it is this: Compassion.

Also, at the end of this collection Per Seyersted has given us a glimpse of Laurence at the end of her life. We learn what she was going through even as this book was being prepared. She was more compassionate than ever; she was faced with a fatal illness; she was hurt by bureaucratic misreadings of her books; she was grateful. It becomes possible to see how she might have received this book had she lived longer, as was the intention at the start. Our purpose was to show that her books are not being misread. They are not being used to further suppression and narrow-mindedness, as the case of book-banning in Ontario schools threatened to represent. To the contrary, her books are sparking some of the finest criticism and thinking that goes on today. Our values—the humanitarian commitment to compassion and excellence—are emphasized and given support. She has been a great guide to all of us. With this collection we wanted to say that yes, indeed, we will endeavour to cross the river about which she speaks in *This Side Jordan*.

Winnipeg, August 1988

CROSSING THE RIVER:
Essays in Honour of Margaret Laurence

Walter E. Swayze
University of Winnipeg

Introduction

Knowing through Writing: The Pilgrimage of Margaret Laurence

SOME OF US knew Margaret personally. We think of her easygoing friendliness; her generosity, whether she was giving or receiving hospitality; her throaty laughter and earthy sense of humour; her incredibly caring interest in her friends and their families; her intense pride in her own family, and especially in her children, Jocelyn and David; her hatred of pretension and her constant unassumingness, paradoxically coupled with an unusual seriousness and sense of responsibility; her frightening shyness which made public appearances terrifying agony; and her total courage in saying anything to anybody if she believed it and believed it had to be said.

To thousands, of course, Margaret Laurence is the writer who has done more than most to establish the importance of writing and to make it possible for others to write, by her own personal example as a woman writer, a prairie writer, and by the example of her own writing, not only in Canada, but in many countries. Chinua Achebe and other Nigerian writers, for example, have repeatedly acknowledged the stimulus and the fostering that she gave to the brilliant literary movement that was so tragically truncated by civil war. But to an incredible number of Canadian writers she has given individual encouragement and generous personal help. Not only did she serve as an active writer-in-residence at Toronto, Trent, and Western Ontario, and participated in writers' workshops, but she regularly wrote to new writers whose work she had read and liked, and made her homes in England and Canada hostels for impecunious writers or for would-be writers suffering from writer's block. She played a leading role in founding the Writers' Union of Canada and chaired the committee that drafted its first constitution. She edited the works of Sinclair Ross, Percy Janes, Jack Ludwig, Adele Wiseman, and others for the New Canadian Library, served on juries for the Governor-General's Awards for several years when she had no books in competition, reviewed dozens of books formally for newspapers from Vancouver to Toronto and for magazines and journals, large and small, and reviewed many other volumes informally for publishers before publication. It would be hard to count the number of books that have appeared with Margaret Laurence's generous praise heading the blurbs on their dust jackets. I won't try to count the number of times she wrote or phoned to say that I should look out for a novel by a new young writer, or the times that she suggested that my subscribing to a new literary periodical would be appreciated. In a recent issue of the *University of Winnipeg Journal* my colleague, Professor Al Reimer, writes eloquently of what her encouragement has meant to him (7).

Hundreds of writers would join us today in celebrating the catholicity of her taste, the generosity of her encouragement of writing frequently quite different from her own, and her unyielding refusal to speak ill of any of her fellow writers. Her tributes to the late William L. Morton, to Clara Thomas, to Adele Wiseman, to George Woodcock, to Lois Wilson and to others, are deservedly well known.

Many of us are not writers, however, and may have no intention of trying to be writers. But we are readers. We represent the many thousands of readers in Canada and around the world, readers of her works translated into several languages and constantly reprinted in a variety of series and formats, readers who may have no interest in academic criticism or concern for the literary establishment, but readers who have read her novels and short stories with gratitude. They have given us a good read, but they have said something important to us, something that has struck home in a significant way.

In introducing a special Margaret Laurence issue of the *Journal of Canadian Studies* a decade ago, Michael Peterman talks about "the positive, larger-than-life image Margaret Laurence projects, the magnetic field she creates around herself." He goes on to say: "For many Canadians she has become an eminence, a wise and generous voice providing insight into, and guidance for, a highly self-conscious nation in the process of reviewing its complicated history and complex character" (2).

In my own words I add that she has become an eminence providing insight and guidance into many areas for many different groups of people, insight into such matters as the relations between imperial powers and subject cultures, relations in the family between the generations, relations between the sexes, between the individual and the past, present, and future, between the individual and the total Not-I that the individual confronts in the mazes of life, coming to terms with loneliness and frustration, with mortality.

The moment one starts to discuss a teaching or prophetic role for an author, one moves into dangerous territory. A few years ago when one of the recurring waves of censorship was rolling over the country, I spoke to a large group of teachers about the use of Margaret Laurence's books in the high school curriculum. Assuming some initial diffidence or even hostility, I tried to demonstrate my conviction that her novels and stories are far from pornographic or cynical, but highly moral and *often* distinctively and penetratingly Christian. When I had finished, more than one member of my audience said in effect, "If she's *that* Christian we couldn't possibly teach her works in our classes, because we have Jews, Moslems, Hindus, agnostics, and atheists, and we can't use sectarian materials that would increase tensions or divisions in our classes."

I don't want to be misunderstood here as I seem to have been misunderstood there. In none of her fiction is Margaret Laurence ever consciously didactic. She is very clear about the autonomy of art, even if art has moral or religious implications. I quote from "My Final Hour," written when she was consciously and intentionally didactic in her non-fiction writing. "My Final Hour" is an address delivered to the Trent University Philosophy Society, March 29, 1983, printed as probably the strongest piece of writing in the 25th Anniversary Issue of *Canadian Literature* in the spring of 1984, and frequently reprinted:

> All art is a product of the human imagination. It is, deeply, an honouring of the past, a perception of the present in one way or another, and a looking towards the future. Whatever the medium of any particular artist, art is reaching out, an attempt to communicate those things which most concern us seriously in our sojourn here on earth. Artists, the real ones, the committed ones, have always sought, sometimes in ways prophetic and beyond their own times, to clarify and proclaim and enhance life, not to obscure and demean and destroy it. Even the so-called literature of despair is not really that at all. Despair is total silence, total withdrawal. Art, by its very nature of necessary expression, is an act of faith, an acknowledgement of the profound mystery at the core of life.
>
> As a writer, therefore, I feel I have a responsibility. Not to write pamphlets, not to write didactic fiction.

> That would be, in many ways, a betrayal of how I feel about my work. But my responsibility seems to me to be to write as truthfully as I can, about human individuals and their dilemmas, to honour them as living, suffering, and sometimes joyful people. (196)

In writing as truthfully as she can about human individuals and their dilemmas, however, Margaret Laurence has discovered or learned ideas and formal convictions which she can express in essays such as "My Final Hour." I choose the words *discovered* or *learned* carefully, however, and they are at the heart of my argument. Patricia Morley, Jane Leney, and others have written persuasively about the way O. Mannoni's *Prospero and Caliban: A Study of the Psychology of Colonization* illuminates the thought patterns of Laurence's African writings, but they admit freely that *This Side Jordan* and many of the stories of *The Tomorrow-Tamer* had probably been written before Laurence had heard of Mannoni. Mannoni confirms in sociological terms what Laurence had already discovered in the process of understanding characters who became real to her when she was writing out of her African experiences.

Similarly, Nancy Bailey's 1977 study of the relation of Laurence's heroines to the thought of Carl Jung does not depend on Laurence's having read Jung before writing much of the fiction discussed in the article. Helen Buss's 1985 monograph, *Mother and Daughter Relationships in the Manawaka Works of Margaret Laurence*, does not depend on Laurence's use of Jung or even of the Demeter-Kore myth, which Buss advances as the prototype of the mother archetype. Kenneth James Hughes' detailed analyses of *A Jest of God* and *The Diviners* as presentations of social and political changes in a developing Canada in Freudian and Marxist terms are learned and ingenious. Margaret Laurence has expressed complete innocence of awareness of the theses that Hughes derives from her works, but Hughes defends them with the words: "If the author's interpretation does not account for all the evidence, and if an opposing interpretation accounts for more evidence, then the latter must take precedence, all other things being equal" (*JCS* 53).

I say these things not to discredit any specific critical discussions of Laurence's ideas; her work has inspired some of the best literary criticism yet written in Canada. But I say these things to emphasize that Margaret Laurence did not start out with ideas and convictions that she wanted to embody in her fiction. In the course of writing that fiction she made discoveries that her readers can isolate and discuss in terms related to critical structures and ideologies of which she may have been unaware until they were pointed out to her. She never studied gerontology or geriatrics, but *The Stone Angel* is required reading in almost every geriatrics program in Canada and in many other countries.

The same may be said for her ideas of fiction. Several times I have asked her what writers she most admired, and she consistently named Joyce Cary, Graham Greene, Patrick White, and E.L. Doctorow. I cannot see evidence of much similarity between any of their works and any of hers. All of her discussions of her own writing, such as "Gadgetry or Growing: Form and Voice in the Novel," concentrate *entirely* on her own experience of writing. As she says so movingly in her 1971 essay, "Where the World Began," her brilliant evocation of Neepawa:

> When I was eighteen, I couldn't wait to get out of that town, away from the prairies. I did not know then that I would carry the land and town all my life within my skull, that they would form the mainspring and source of the writing I was to do, wherever and however far away I might live. (*HS* 217)
>
> ....
>
> This is where my world began. A world which includes the ancestors—both my own and other people's ancestors who became mine. A world which formed me,

> and continues to do so, even while I fought it in some of its aspects, and continue to do so. A world which gave me my own lifework to do, because it was here that I learned the sight of my own particular eyes. (*HS* 219)

Margaret Laurence maintained a library that most scholars would envy. She always read widely and deeply. But she learned far more from the sight of her own particular eyes than she did from other people's books, and her knowledge came especially from her own writing.

Take her Christianity, for example. Her family background was at least nominally religious and she certainly grew up in an environment of Biblical allusion and normal church attendance. She attended United College, and was close friends with many theological students. But her fictional childhood counterparts, Vanessa MacLeod and Morag Gunn, do not seem particularly satisfied with the standard orthodoxies of church and Sunday School, nor do her adult characters, Rachel Cameron, Stacey MacAindra, and Hagar Shipley. As Laurence says in *The Prophet's Camel Bell*, it wasn't until she was a married woman en route to Somaliland that, frustrated with a lack of reading material, she paced her hotel room until she discovered the Gideon Bible in a dressing-table drawer and for the first time in her life read the five books of Moses right through (9). From her first adult story, "The Drummer of All the World" (1956), to her last novel, *The Diviners* (1974), her fictional characters are usually violently (to some readers, blasphemously) critical of the behaviour and the intelligence of most conforming Christians and critical of most conventional Christian observances. They are oppressed with the enslaving rigidity and the absurdity of most religious beliefs. Yet all of these characters at moments of abject hopelessness experience what seem to be Christian illuminations and gain a sense of freedom and strength to go on confidently, even joyously.

After the publication of *The Diviners*, when Christian

ministers were preaching sermons on her work and inviting her to participate in worship services, just as Molière's M. Jourdain discovered to his delight that he was able to speak prose, Margaret Laurence realized, not that she had been using Biblical allusions in her fiction and that Christmas had been from her childhood a celebration of love, but that most of her convictions were Christian, that she really believed in Divine Grace, and that she wanted to join publicly in Christian worship in her local community. This is an oversimplification, of course, but let me illustrate with a few examples.

The young Hagar Currie in *The Stone Angel* is scornful of her father's regular attendance at Sunday service and his grace at meals, contemptuous of the tiny plaques on the silver candlesticks at the front of the church bearing her father's name, the purchased pew "furnished with long cushions of brown and beige velour, so [that their] few favored bottoms would not be bothered by hard oak and a lengthy sermon," her father's pride in the inference that he and "Luke McVitie must've given the most" from the fact that the minister called their names first when acknowledging the "generosity and Christian contributions" that made the new church possible (15-16). The old Hagar is rudely contemptuous of Doris' minister, Mr. Troy, and Mr. Troy is embarrassed at his failure when he has been most successful. When Mr. Troy asks her if she doesn't believe in God's infinite Mercy, Hagar replies, "What's so merciful about Him, I'd like to know?"

> "I had a son," I say, "and lost him."
> "You're not alone," says Mr. Troy.
> "That's where you're wrong," I reply. (120-21)

The Christian reader, of course, knows that God had a Son, and lost Him. By the end of the novel, after a life wasted by blinding, joyless pride, Hagar realizes this after trying to embarrass Mr. Troy by getting him to attempt to sing "Old

Hundredth." Her humbling of her pride to tell Marvin in love that he's been a good son, better than John, gives her, she says, "more than I could now reasonably have expected out of life." Her risking of her own life to get the bed pan for young Sandra Wong is at least the equivalent of giving a cup of cold water; and in her last moment of life Hagar wrests from the nurse her "glass, full of water to be had for the taking," in an action that suggests the usual sacramental symbolism of grace, and recalls the glass of water she had wanted in the abandoned cannery when she had had the frightening vision of the ocean as infinite time, space, and life, from which people were protected only by human companionship (224-25, 250). Like King Lear, she learns too late, but her learning at all establishes for her and for the reader the reality of the order that she has resisted all her life and the obligation to rejoice in it.

Characters younger than Hagar learn much earlier, though not necessarily less painfully or more easily. Rachel Cameron in *A Jest of God* is contemptuous of her mother's religion:

> She loves coming to church because she sees everyone, and in spring the new hats are like a forest of tulips. But as for faith—I suppose she takes it for granted that she believes. Yet if the Reverend MacElfish should suddenly lose his mind and speak of God with anguish or joy, or out of some need should pray with fierce humility as though God had to be there, Mother would be shocked to the core. Luckily, it will never happen. (41)

Rachel is constantly protesting to God and attacking Him and pleading with Him, all in quick succession. At one point, she says, "If I believed, I would have to detest God for the brutal joker He would be if He existed" (42). But having been the target of a brutal joke, having had a tumour just when she had come to terms with having an illegitimate child that would have utterly disgraced her in the community, having been made a fool in various ways, she becomes wise. When her mother accuses her of heartlessly risking her life, Rachel says,

> "Well, in the end—the end—it's in other hands."
>
> I've spoken so oddly and ambiguously, not knowing I was going to deliver this nineteenth-century cliché until I heard it. . . . And yet, what I said was also meant, unintentionally intended. . . . It isn't up to me. It never was. I can take care, but only some. . . . There is, suddenly, some enormous relief in this realization. (194-95)

And hence, after this moment of grace, Rachel is strong enough to trust life and to set out heroically against all odds. Her last line is: "God's mercy on reluctant jesters. God's grace on fools, God's pity on God." This is not the God of Hagar's father nor of Rachel's mother. But this is the God who suffers along with his stubborn, rebellious, insensitive, unimaginative creatures, the God who suffers the infinite pain of all creation, but who gives grace sufficient to those who need it when they need it.

Rachel's sister, Stacey MacAindra, in *The Fire-Dwellers*, is even more caustically contemptuous of standard Christian doctrines and practices, and argues constantly and violently with God in her soliloquies:

> Listen here, God, don't talk to me like that. You have no right. *You* try bringing up four kids. . . . So next time you send somebody down here, get It born as a her with seven young or a him with a large family and a rotten boss, eh? Then we'll see how the inspirational bit goes. (168)

Her father-in-law Matthew, a retired ordained minister, has little conviction or confidence in his belief and little comfort from it. But by the end of the novel, after years of loneliness and guilt-ridden frustration, in a world in which children can be killed by automobiles or almost drowned while swimming, or blasted by police bullets or burned with napalm, in which the threat of nuclear destruction seems imminent, Stacey is still able to hope and dream, and is given the grace to go on. "Temporarily," she says as she slides into sleep, "they are all more or less okay" (308).

By the end of the eight short stories of *A Bird in the House,* Vanessa MacLeod, after experiences as rebellious and potentially tragic as those of the heroines of the novels, has come to terms with herself and the qualities of her heritage that she has hated throughout most of her life, and also with her own mortality, and presumably is able to go on confidently as a person and as a writer.

About *The Diviners*, the author repeatedly has said that Christie Logan's name is not accidental, and his function is unmistakable. As John the Baptist said of Christ, "Behold the Lamb of God, which taketh away the sin of the world!" (KJV John 1:29), Christie takes away the garbage of Manawaka and keeps the nuisance grounds. His vigorous cataloguing of the garbage and his interpretation of the lives and values of the community in his divination are both too well known to need quoting. Like the Suffering Servant in Isaiah 53:3, "He is despised and rejected of men; a man of sorrows, and acquainted with grief; and we hid as it were our faces from him; he was despised, and we esteemed him not" (KJV). And yet it is Christie who provides the fostering care for the orphan Morag, and who by his intimate knowledge of people gives her the knowledge that is to make her the writer, and by his rhapsodic Ossianic tales of Piper Gunn tells her who she is, where she comes from, what values she inherits. His death and burial are among the tenderest and most triumphant scenes in literature. Yet the symbolism of Christie Logan is inextricably woven into the incredibly rich texture of this whole novel. The whole experience of Morag Gunn is as circumstantially vivid as the details of Dante's *Divine Comedy*, and the conclusion is as triumphantly Christian. The miracle of saving grace is mirrored in the miracle of writing, which makes a novel such as *The Diviners* emerge out of the writer's subconscious, or unconscious, beyond the control of her will. Not until the novel is finished can Morag Gunn or Margaret Laurence set down her title that helps to define the thrust of the novel.

I saw Margaret Laurence several times, in England and in Canada, when she was struggling with *The Diviners*. I know that she did not set out to write a Christian novel and was not conscious that she was writing one until it was almost finished. She was struggling with characters who had much in common with herself and people she knew, and in coming to a realization of the shape of Morag Gunn's experience, she came to understand her own. Her characters' realizations became her illuminations—and ours.

What is true of Laurence's religious insights is true of all her others. Her 1966 article "Road from the Isles" is, as she says, "an early working out in non-fiction, of a theme I would later, in *The Diviners*, express in fiction," namely, the feeling that she had when making a pilgrimage to the land of her ancestors and then finding out where she really came from and where she really belonged. But the experience of Morag Gunn in *The Diviners* is far richer than the earlier experience of Margaret Laurence in this preliminary essay.

In "The Decay of Lying" Oscar Wilde at his most brilliant argues that Life imitates Art, that the best sunsets copy the best Turners of Turner's best period, that the fogs on the Thames imitate the Impressionists. Beneath the witty, superficial inversions of clichés Wilde is arguing seriously that Nature doesn't really exist for us until the artistic imagination has made us aware of it. To apply this concept to Margaret Laurence we can see very clearly why she gave us no novels after *The Diviners*, just a volume of essays, many of which had been written earlier, three children's books, one of which had been written many years earlier, and many addresses, articles, pamphlets, and letters in support of such causes as Energy Probe and Project Ploughshares.

Twice since the publication of *The Diviners* Margaret cancelled proposed visits to Winnipeg because she was, as she put it, being given a new novel, and did not want to interrupt the flow while it was being given. She always refused to discuss what she was writing until she was certain that it was nearly finished. However, in 1978, when at her request I had driven her around the old North End to visit several Ukrainian sites, starting out from the Ukrainian Labor Temple on Pritchard Avenue, I couldn't help speculating that her experience as labour reporter on the Winnipeg *Citizen* when she lived on Burrows Avenue just after her marriage might at last be bearing fruit in a novel that would bring the Kazliks of *A Jest of God* into focus the way *The Diviners* had brought to rich fulfillment the hints of the Tonnerre Métis experience from *The Stone Angel, The Fire-Dwellers*, and "The Loons" in *A Bird in the House*. And Margaret did tell Robert Kroetsch that she had been "given" a novel, presumably on the Selkirk Settlers, again presumably developing the stories that Christie Logan told Morag in *The Diviners*. But neither novel was ever mentioned again.

In *The Fire-Dwellers* (1969), Stacey, in great distress, says to Luke:

> There was this newspaper picture of this boy some city in the States   kid about twelve   Negro kid   you know   shot by accident   it said by the police in a riot and he was just lying there not dead but lying with his arm cradled up in a dark pool   his blood and his eyes were wide open   and you wondered what he was seeing. His parents cared about him as much as I do about my kids, no doubt, and worried about what might happen to him, but that didn't stop it happening. You think I'm silly to think about   I can't help it (193)

A few months earlier, in terms of publication, though probably later in terms of writing, in "Open Letter to the Mother of Joe Bass," published in Al Purdy's *The New Romans*, and reprinted in *Heart of a Stranger*, Margaret Laurence elaborates the relation of this newspaper picture to her own son, David:

> I have seen your son only once, Mrs. Bass. That was in a newspaper photograph. In Detroit, he went out one evening when his playmates asked him to. It was not an evening to be out. Your son was shot by the police. By accident, the paper said. Shot by accident in the neck. The police were aiming at Billy Furr, who was walking out of Mack Liquors, not with a fortune in his hands but with precisely six tins of stolen beer. When Billy Furr saw the police, something told him to run and keep on running, so he did that, and he was shot dead. But the police had fired more than once, and Joe Bass happened to be in the way. The papers did not say whether he was expected to recover or not, nor how much a twelve-year-old could recover from something like that. A Negro twelve-year-old.
>
> Your son looked a skinny kid, a little taller than my twelve-year-old but not as robust. He was lying on the sidewalk, and his eyes were open. He was seeing everything, I guess, including himself. He was bleeding, and one of his hands lay languidly outstretched in a spillage of blood. His face didn't have any expression at all. I looked at the picture for quite a long time. Then I put it away, but it would not be put away. The blank kid-face there kept fluctuating in my mind. Sometimes it was the face of your son, sometimes of mine.
>
> Then I recalled another newspaper photograph. It was of a North Vietnamese woman. Some marvelous new kind of napalm had just come into use. I do not understand the technicalities. This substance when it alights flaming onto skin cannot be removed. It adheres. The woman was holding a child who looked about eighteen months old, and she was trying to pluck something away from the burn-blackening area on the child's face. I wondered how she felt when her child newly took

> on life and emerged, and if she had almost imagined she was looking over God's shoulder then.
>
> I have spent fifteen years of my life writing novels and other things. I have had, if any faith at all, a faith in the word. *In the beginning was the Word, and the Word was with God, and the Word was God.* The kind of belief that many writers have—the belief that if we are to make ourselves known to one another, if we are really to know the reality of another, we must communicate with what is almost the only means we have—human speech. There are other means of communication, I know, but they are limited because they are so personal and individual—we can make love; we can hold and comfort our children. Otherwise, we are stuck with words. We have to try to talk to one another, because this imperfect means is the only general one we have.
>
> And yet—I look at the picture of your twelve-year-old son on the sidewalks of Detroit, pillowed in blood. And I wonder—if it were in physical fact *my* son, of the same age, would I be able to go on writing novels, in the belief that this was a worthwhile thing to be doing in this year (as they say) of Our Lord? Mrs. Bass, I do not think I can answer that question.
>
> I am afraid for all our children. (37)

I was afraid when I read this in 1968. I didn't like it. It made me fear that we might never again see a novel by Margaret Laurence. We did see one, her richest, most technically sophisticated and accomplished, *The Diviners*. But the writing of it almost killed her. Since then we have had loving celebrations of the solidarity of the family in *Six Darn Cows* (1979), the linking of the generations in love and understanding in *The Olden Days Coat* (1979), and the mystery of Divine Love in every human birth and the sacredness of life in *The Christmas Birthday Story* (1980). Margaret inscribed a gift copy of the latter with the words "To Walter and Margaret—and their children—and their children's children—with love." From then on, apart from answering personally well over twelve hundred letters a year, promoting a number of local causes she believed in, and fighting for the right of our children to an education that is not crippled and sterilized by censorship, she has devoted most of her imagination, skill, and energy to doing what she could to ensure that we consider the importance of having a planet on which it is possible to have children and grandchildren, and on which life and love may still flourish.

In 1964 *Tamarack Review* printed Margaret Laurence's short story "A Queen in Thebes." It was never included in a collection of her stories, since it did not fit in with her African stories or her Vanessa MacLeod stories. Its lack of recognition has really nothing to do with its quality. It is simply too horrible for most readers and critics.

A young husband leaves his wife and their baby boy at a remote wilderness summer cottage, with enough firewood for a week, and goes back to the city to work. A nuclear explosion wipes out the husband along with everyone else. Determined to survive, the woman becomes a combination of Robinson Crusoe and Pincher Martin and painfully learns all the techniques required for survival; eventually, after many years, she seems to be doing well:

> The sun of late spring warmed her, and the raw trilling of frogs from the lake made her feel glad, for this was a good time of year, with hunger gone. The fish and game were plentiful, and the roots and leaves of the dandelions were succulent and tender. (50)

But she and her teenage son are troubled by voices from the past, and the story comes to a sudden end:

> She half shut her eyes, and listened intently, but still she could not understand and could only feel troubled by something untouchable, some mystery that remained just beyond her grasp.

> Then, inside the cave, one of the children began crying, and she went to give comfort. (51)

Incest is probably the absolute taboo in most societies. But here, as in *Oedipus Rex* and several other of the greatest tragedies in literature, it is not only frightening, but apparently inevitable. The horror of the ending is what has frightened off most readers who are not prepared to have this little girl from Neepawa open up the depths of a Sophocles, a Racine, a Shakespeare in front of their unthinking tread. But which is more obscene—an act essential to the continuation of human life in the universe or the bureaucratic annihilation of millions of mothers, fathers and children, many of whom have some chance of experiencing Love in their normal relationships?

Eventually Margaret's frightening knowledge of the implications of the experience of the nameless mother in "A Queen in Thebes" and of the mother of Joe Bass made it virtually impossible for her to write fiction. Like Milton, who gave up poetry for twenty years and turned to left-handed prose because the times made any other choice impossible for him, Margaret Laurence set the writing of fiction on the back burner while she gave addresses, wrote pamphlets and letters, and involved herself in the actual management of crusades. In all fairness I must add that she also served as Chancellor of Trent University and that she was almost blind until she had her cataract operation, and for months, was almost unable to move without intense pain from back spasms or to write or type because of pinched nerves in her wrists. Unlike Milton, she was not spared to return to her original calling and give us the prose equivalent of *Paradise Lost, Paradise Regained*, and *Samson Agonistes,* unless, of course, the book completed days before she died could turn out to be the equivalent.

It is appropriate that Margaret Laurence's first honorary degree was the Honorary Fellowship that she received from

United College in October, 1966, and that her last was the doctorate that she received from the University of Manitoba May 27, 1986.

Margaret was always extremely nervous about public appearances, and she seemed more nervous than usual about this last convocation. Yet she was in good spirits, seemed to be in better health than she had been in for several years, and was happy to be with so many old and good friends. In spite of her reluctance to be honoured publicly, she was delighted to be recognized by her own province and by the university of which United College had been a part when she was an undergraduate. She rose to the occasion, literally and figuratively, and although she was afraid she might not be able to stand by herself to receive the degree and to deliver the convocation address, and had made arrangements for assistance if she needed it, she spoke strongly and movingly, more as a prophet than as a writer of fiction, presenting concisely and unerringly the essence of her faith. She handed me the text of what she said, and I share it with you without apology:

> I graduated from this university, having attended one of its then-colleges, United College, nearly forty years ago. My generation was the first ever to emerge from university knowing that the human race now had the terrible ability to destroy the whole human race and all life on earth. I graduated in 1947. In 1945, the first nuclear bombs had been dropped on Hiroshima and Nagasaki. We knew that our earth would never be the same again. We went on, did our work, bore and raised our children, but we have never forgotten that we live under that shadow, and it has shaped our lives in many ways. You are graduating into an even more terrifying world. Injustice, homelessness, starvation, thirst, racism, preventable diseases, pollution of air and water—these are rife in our world, and many are known increasingly here in our country. More than anything, the threat of nuclear war hangs over us all. Both

superpowers, fearful and suspicious of one another, now have enough nuclear arms to destroy all life on earth several times over. Hundreds of billions of dollars are spent, world-wide, every year, on nuclear arms, while less and less is spent on aid to the poor, the disadvantaged, the elderly, and children. Ours is a world in which it is difficult not to feel depressed or indeed hopeless. What I want to say to you today is that we cannot afford to feel hopeless; we cannot afford the debilitating luxury of despair or apathy. We are citizens not only of our own country but of the world. I believe with all my heart that we must do our own work with all devotion, and we must also struggle in the causes of peace and social justice. I make one plea to you—the passionate plea of caring. In your life's work, whatever it may be, live as though you had forever, for no amount of devotion is too great in doing the work to which you have set your hands. Cultivate in your work and your lives the art of patience, and come to terms with your inevitable human limitations, while striving to extend the boundaries of your understanding and compassion. Learn from those older than you are; learn from your contemporaries; never cease to learn from children. Try to know in your heart's core the reality of others. In times of adversity, know that you are not alone. Know that in the eternal scheme of things you are small but you are also unique and irreplaceable, as are all humans everywhere. Know that your commitment is above all to life itself. Your own life and work and loves will someday come to an end, but life and work and love will go on, in your inheritors. The struggle for peace and social justice will go on, provided that caring humans still live. It is up to you now, to do all you can in your own chosen work, and also, at this perilous time in human history, to do all you can to ensure that life itself will go on.

You are among my inheritors. I give you my deepest blessings, my hope and my faith.

When she concluded this address with her blessing to the graduands, the deeply moved response of all present showed how appropriate her blessing was. None of us knew that it was also prophetic, that within a few months, like John Bunyan's Mr. Greatheart, she would have passed over, and all the trumpets would have sounded for her. They continue to sound in our hearing. Her pilgrim's progress is complete. But I still hear her voice saying to me and to all of us what the frightened Nathaniel Amegbe said to his new-born son, just as the new nation of Ghana was being born, in the closing lines of her first novel, *This Side Jordan*:

> "Joshua, Joshua, Joshua. I beg you. Cross Jordan, Joshua." (282)

Works Consulted

Achebe, Chinua. *Morning Yet on Creation Days: Essays*. London: Heinemann Educational Books, 1975.

Bailey, Nancy. "Margaret Laurence, Carl Jung, and the Manawaka Women." *Studies in Canadian Literature* 2.2 (1977): 306-21.

Buss, Helen M. *Mother and Daughter Relationships in the Manawaka Works of Margaret Laurence*. Victoria, B.C.: University of Victoria, 1985.

Hughes, Kenneth James. "Politics and *A Jest of God*." *Journal of Canadian Studies* 13.3 (1978): 40-54.

Laurence, Margaret. *A Bird in the House*. Toronto: McClelland and Stewart, 1970.

__________. *The Christmas Birthday Story*. Toronto: McClelland and Stewart, 1980.

__________. Convocation Address, University of Manitoba, May 27, 1986. Typescript.

__________. "Drummer of All the World." *Queen's Quarterly* 63 (1956): 487-504.

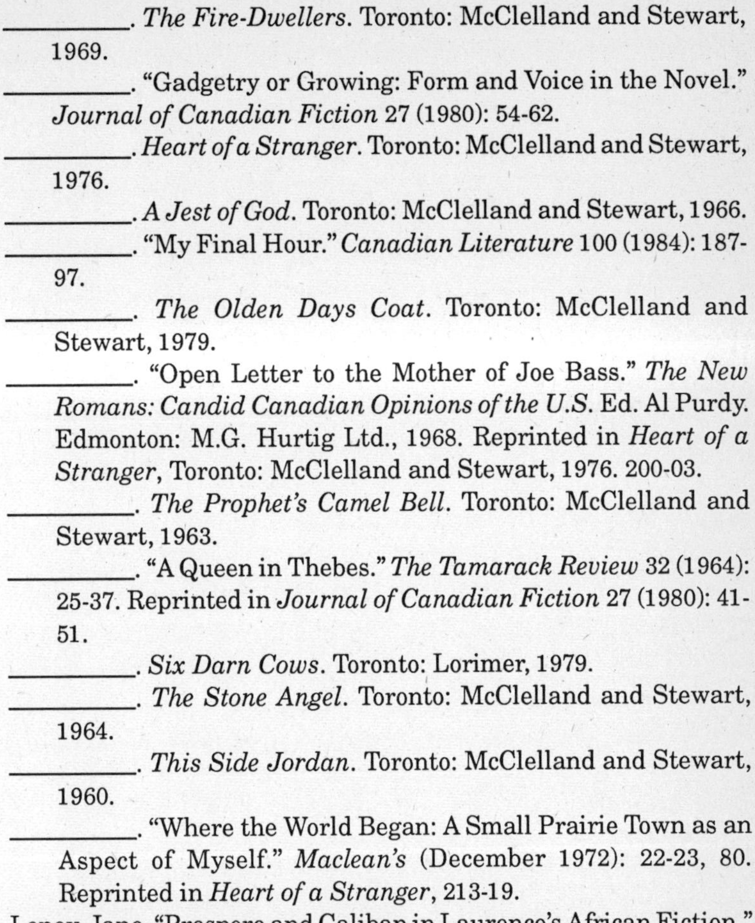

________. *The Fire-Dwellers*. Toronto: McClelland and Stewart, 1969.

________. "Gadgetry or Growing: Form and Voice in the Novel." *Journal of Canadian Fiction* 27 (1980): 54-62.

________. *Heart of a Stranger*. Toronto: McClelland and Stewart, 1976.

________. *A Jest of God*. Toronto: McClelland and Stewart, 1966.

________. "My Final Hour." *Canadian Literature* 100 (1984): 187-97.

________. *The Olden Days Coat*. Toronto: McClelland and Stewart, 1979.

________. "Open Letter to the Mother of Joe Bass." *The New Romans: Candid Canadian Opinions of the U.S.* Ed. Al Purdy. Edmonton: M.G. Hurtig Ltd., 1968. Reprinted in *Heart of a Stranger*, Toronto: McClelland and Stewart, 1976. 200-03.

________. *The Prophet's Camel Bell*. Toronto: McClelland and Stewart, 1963.

________. "A Queen in Thebes." *The Tamarack Review* 32 (1964): 25-37. Reprinted in *Journal of Canadian Fiction* 27 (1980): 41-51.

________. *Six Darn Cows*. Toronto: Lorimer, 1979.

________. *The Stone Angel*. Toronto: McClelland and Stewart, 1964.

________. *This Side Jordan*. Toronto: McClelland and Stewart, 1960.

________. "Where the World Began: A Small Prairie Town as an Aspect of Myself." *Maclean's* (December 1972): 22-23, 80. Reprinted in *Heart of a Stranger*, 213-19.

Leney, Jane. "Prospero and Caliban in Laurence's African Fiction." *Journal of Canadian Studies* 27 (1980): 63-80.

Morley, Patricia. "Margaret Laurence's Early Writing: a world in which Others have to be respected." *Journal of Canadian Studies* 13.3 (1978): 13-18.

Peterman, Michael. "Margaret Laurence." *Journal of Canadian Studies* 13.3 (1978): 1-2, 100-04.

Reimer, Al. "The Spirit of Margaret Laurence." *University of Winnipeg Journal* 3.2 (1987): 7.

Constance Rooke
University of Guelph

Hagar's Old Age: *The Stone Angel* as *Vollendungsroman*

"AND THEN—" *The Stone Angel* closes, signalling the instant of Hagar's death, and the conundrum of its sequel, and one further pressing question—which is whether (in fictional terms) Hagar will live on. *The Stone Angel*, an act of imagination performed by Margaret Laurence, is completed with those words; "and then—" it's up to us, her readers and heirs, to say whether Laurence has pulled it off, her own implicit goal, which is to confer immortality upon a thing made out of words. And I refer here to Hagar, rather than to the novel which contains and shapes her. Immortality is paradoxically achieved if we are made to see the character as something *more* than words; the trick that Laurence attempts (with words that last) is to make her seem like flesh and blood, perishable and poignant beyond words for just that reason.

Clearly, the trick has worked. In Canadian literature, Hagar is reigning still as Queen of all the characters. Even critics who are theoretically bound to recall that any character is really only a linguistic construct—a series of characters, in the alphabetical sense—may slip and fall into the heresy of the real where Hagar is concerned. What I shall be arguing in this essay is that Hagar's peculiarly strong 'reality' quotient is a function of her pressing *need* for some version of continuance, some species of immortality. We find ourselves compelled—by language, for how else can any case be argued?—to grant her what we can. Further, I would suggest that Hagar's need is a function of her old age, as the proximity of death and the spectacle of ninety misspent years demand *riposte*.

In an essay called "Gadgetry or Growing: Form and Voice in the Novel," Margaret Laurence defined herself as a writer whose fate or task or vocation was the creation of character. And Laurence was inclined, always, to speak of her characters as if they were real, as if they were people to whom she owed something, as if they had rights that could be violated by a careless author. That authorial stance is familiar enough. But Laurence—as if intoning Hagar's famous battle-cry, "Gainsay Who Dare!"—stood her ground with remarkable firmness: "Form for its own sake is an abstraction which carries no allure for me" (55). What she sought was "a form which would allow the characters to come through" (54), "a form through which the characters can breathe" (55). Laurence's job, as she construed it, was to listen well to their voices and to devise a structure in which her characters would appear to "breathe," a kind of hospitable, open-air auditorium in which their stories might be told and heard.

I am interested in the visual metaphor that Laurence found when she tried to describe her ideal form: "a forest, through which one can see outward, in which the shapes of trees do not prevent air and sun, and in which the trees themselves are growing structures, something alive" (55). What seems to be at work here is the revision and reversal of an old cliché. We should not be prevented from seeing out of the forest by the trees; that is, the elements of form must not obscure our vision of that reality which lies beyond form—

and animates it. And we should not be prevented from seeing the trees by the forest; that is, the form as a whole (a finished abstraction, the book or forest) must not obscure our vision of that reality which continues to grow and change within it.

But I am also interested in the metaphors of form that Laurence excluded in the essay called "Gadgetry or Growing": "I see it not like a house or a cathedral or any enclosing edifice, but rather as a forest." Her concern, it seems, is to discover a form in which characters can breathe fresh air. And I think this follows from her interest in the dialectic between fixed or rooted elements of the human personality and the winds of change. She wants her characters to breathe not only in the sense of coming to life, and transcending the "gadgetry" of form, but also in the sense of "growing." Her exclusion of the metaphor of the house has a special bearing on the topic of Hagar's old age—because Hagar has throughout her life made the mistake of identifying her self with that "enclosing edifice." In old age, and in the "growing" form of the novel that Laurence discovers for her, Hagar is able at last to emerge from the carapace of her "house." It is only in this departure from her accustomed form that Hagar can achieve the immortality of characters who are "growing" still in the last chapter.

"Gadgetry or Growing" is also the essay in which Laurence spoke of her uncertainty over the chronological ordering of Hagar's memory and the 'poetic' quality of her voice. Laurence's question was whether the methods she had chosen "diminish[ed] the novel's resemblance to life" (56). On the memory issue, she defended her choice by suggesting that a more apparently haphazard arrangement might have confused the reader, and that in any case "writing—however consciously unordered its method—is never as disorderly as life. Art, in fact, is never life. It is never as paradoxical, chaotic, complex or as alive as life" (56-57). I think, in fact, that Laurence was right in her assessment that "the novel is probably too orderly." But there is another argument that can be made, one that proceeds from her reminder that art is never life, one that seizes upon the difference—not to excuse the gap, but to exploit it.

The Stone Angel is a novel. We know that as we read, and we know absolutely that it is an attempt by Margaret Laurence to redeem or perform a salvage operation on a character who means a great deal to her. The text is an arena in which Laurence exercises both her skill and her love—for this imagined person, for whatever real persons may have contributed to the invention of Hagar, and for the human enterprise. I would argue that a significant factor in our admiration or love for this novel is the *presence* of Laurence, accomplishing through art the feat of human salvage; the river flows both ways, and we associate Margaret Laurence's triumph (the struggle and reach of her imagination) with Hagar's own emancipation, so that each extends a kind of grace or power to the other.

So Hagar's memories are invoked in chronological order; moreover, each memory is interrupted by a present event only when the past segment has yielded its relevant content. The effect of all this is to remind us of artifice, for good or ill. The threat to realism is contained by various artful dodges, including the credible triggers for memory which propel Hagar from the present into the past. A notable and complex example occurs in the woods at Shadow Point, where Hagar sees the sparrows as "jurors [who would] condemn [her] quick as a wink, no doubt" (192), and then remembers the locus of her 'crime', the scene in which she and Lottie had plotted to separate their children. Because this is a particularly long segment, Laurence also gives us a clump of moss and a blind slug which are sounded fore and aft to frame the memory; these are natural, probable signposts, to be sure—but they are also mutedly symbolic, and artful. (We feel the slowness of time, the long repression of dangerous psychic material.)

I have chosen this example—rather than, say, the paintings in the doctor's office that cause Hagar to recall pictures hung at the Shipley place—because, while the trigger here is not straightforward, it is credible in spite of the artfulness imputed to Hagar herself. We might say that the moss and slug are Laurence's doing, and that the judgement parallel is Hagar's. But in fact some slippage occurs in both directions, and we understand that Hagar is not unlike her author in the need to tease out and shape the meanings of her material. Memory *is* an art. It becomes more potent as Hagar becomes more skilled in the integration of past and present, as she learns from each how to learn from the other; and she educates herself, with the assistance of her author, partly through the manipulation of symbol.

Therefore I would argue that the gap between art and life which is revealed to Laurence by the necessarily greater disorder of life is a dynamic gap; from the energy that crosses to and fro both are enriched. If *The Stone Angel* can be criticized for an excessive orderliness—and I would extend the charge beyond the matter of chronological memory, to include an excessively orderly (or over-resolved) handling of image—this is clearly not a fatal flaw. The novel is splendid in any case. And it is splendid partly because art and life, or the author and the character, are allowed to reflect each other passionately across that gap.

I have been dealing here surreptitiously with the question of Hagar's 'poetic' voice, which Laurence also addresses in "Gadgetry or Growing" as a possible lapse in verisimilitude. On this point, however, she is more confident. Laurence begins by recalling her anxiety when she read over certain of Hagar's more elaborate or 'poetic' descriptions: "Were these in fact Hagar or were they me? I worried about this quite a lot, because I did not want Hagar to think out of character" (57). But she justifies her decision to let this voice stand by appealing to her sense of conviction in the writing—"I could not really believe those descriptions *were* out of character"—and to the notion that rescinding them "would be a kind of insult" to Hagar. She argues further that "even people who are relatively inarticulate . . . are perfectly capable within themselves of perceiving the world in more poetic terms . . . than their outer voices might indicate."

This defense suggests Laurence's fervent advocacy of her character, her need to take Hagar's side and to arm her as fully as their shared humanity permits. I would accept the spirit of her contention that the inner voice can be more articulate or 'poetic' than the outer, but Hagar's voice—with its high degree of rhetorical polish, even in the vernacular—is nonetheless very clearly a literary construct. I am not troubled by this fact, however; I *like* it. The effect of Hagar's very literary panache is not of self-consciousness on her author's part, but rather of a desire (shared by author and character) that Hagar should express herself as well and as fully as possible before the lights go out.

W.H. New, in an essay called "Every Now and Then: Voice and Language in Laurence's *The Stone Angel*," discusses "the *writerly* quality of the language with which Hagar constructs the world" (81) and suggests (what is clearly so) that the tension between her formal and vernacular styles of speech reflects a social tension within both Hagar and her world. Where I differ from New is in his suggestion that Hagar's formal or "finishing school" voice is reducible to the enemy within, which has protected and distracted her from truths of the body and ordinary life that "come during the passages of uncontrolled utterance, when the *natural* Hagar can be heard" (92). New recognizes that the "natural," anti-hierarchical Hagar is also posited in the abundant natural imagery of even her most formal speech; but I think he romanticizes the "natural" and the inarticulate, and dismisses too much of what is valuable in Hagar's character, when he suggests that the elaborate *style* of such passages is simply Hagar's way of "distanc[ing] herself from life" (90). To pursue the evident social tensions in her language this far is to run the risk of despising Hagar's eloquence.

I am reminded of Margaret Laurence's fear that to censor Hagar's 'poetic' voice "would be a kind of insult to her. And that, I wasn't willing to risk—indeed I did not dare" (Gadgetry 57). In deciding to trust that voice as Hagar's own, Laurence appealed to the truth of the subconscious—from which all writing partly comes, and in which the character is born; it would seem, then, that Laurence herself believed in the spiritual authenticity of Hagar's educated voice. The mistake that New makes, in my opinion, is to accept too literally or too purely the fictional proposition that Hagar's voice is that of a 'real' person. Its modulations are therefore regarded precisely as if they had been transcribed from life, and Hagar is held strictly accountable for them all. This credulity leads the critic astray, whereas the novelist's brand of poetic faith in the 'reality' of her character allows Margaret Laurence to speak for Hagar with conviction—and to negotiate with impunity the gap between life and art.

My concern here with the interplay of life and art, and of the character with her author, is a necessary approach to the main topic of this essay, which is *The Stone Angel* as a novel 'about' old age. I have been studying such novels for several years now, and have coined a term by which to refer to them: the *Vollendungsroman*, the novel of "completion" or "winding up." *The Stone Angel* has become my central or prototypical example of the genre, for a number of reasons that I shall be sketching here. The least provable of these is also one of the most compelling: that I sense generally in the *Vollendungsroman*, and with great force in *The Stone Angel*, a kind of alliance between the elderly character and the author—as language itself becomes the agent of affirmation.

A special intensity (resulting from the proximity to darkness) characterizes the *Vollendungsroman*. The writer's imagination—I would suggest—is challenged by the prospect of the character's demise, and by the need to 'capture' a life before it vanishes. Behind this, and quite apart from the question of the author's own age, is undoubtedly the spectre of the writer's own aging and prospective death. Writing is always an act directed against death; it may become that more specifically and more urgently when the writer's subject is old age. Thus, we feel strongly the need that Laurence feels to let her elderly protagonist *speak* "before [her] mouth is stopped with dark" (139).

The act of speech operates in the *Vollendungsroman* in several ways. Broadly or metaphorically speaking, it is all of the *writing* performed on the protagonist's behalf by the novelist; more literally, it includes the inner (silent) discourse of the protagonist; finally, of course, it is all speech performed out loud by the elderly protagonist. Speech of this most literal kind may be divided further. Often, there is something that must be said to other characters, in order to free them for their own lives; this is illustrated by Hagar's statement to Marvin that he has been " 'good to [her], always. A better son than John' " (304). And it is typical of the *Vollendungsroman* that the truth of this crucial speech act should be in question; what matters is that the thing be said, the gist of it, before the power of speech is gone. An imprecise formulation—even a lie, though Hagar speaks more truly than she knows—is not only preferable to silence, but all that can be hoped for. If Hagar fails "to speak the heart's truth" (292), she fails in part because we all necessarily fail—and because language fails, always.

Still it is what we have. Through language, we communicate some portion or version of "the heart's truth" and so become visible, assuming a more or less reliable shape in one another's eyes—so that Marvin, in his turn, can remark to the nurse that his mother is "a holy terror" (304), and Hagar can feel this accolade as "more than [she] could . . . reasonably have expected out of life, for he has spoken with such anger and such tenderness" (305). However imperfectly, Hagar and Marvin connect *in time* through language. Such moments have a heightened importance in the *Vollendungsroman*, where time is running out.

It is also characteristic of the *Vollendungsroman* that the elderly protagonist is tormented by the memory of characters who have died before some vital message could be delivered or received. Thus, Hagar wants Bram to know she loved him and wants John to know that she regrets the plot to separate him from Arlene. And it is too late. But *The Stone Angel*, like other *Vollendungsromans*, supplies amelioration through delayed and displaced speech, as figures like Murray Lees appear to take the words that Hagar needs to give. None of this can change the damage she has done to others in the past; "Nothing can take away those years" (292), as Hagar knows full well, unleashing the savage irony that she hears in the minister's words of comfort. Yet language can begin to repair the damage Hagar has done to herself. Speech acts, exchanged with surrogate figures, help her to see what might have been and what she is capable of being even now. They collapse time even as they enforce its tragic necessity, and reveal to Hagar her continuing potential for connectedness in the human family. They point both to the past in which she might have spoken thus, and to the present in which she does.

Hagar thinks that she is "unchangeable, unregenerate. I go on speaking in the same way, always" (293); thus, her problem with speech is as much with what she says as what she fails to say; and her problem is that in both ways she separates herself from others. Following this self-accusation, however, Hagar withdraws her dismissive remark about the minister—" 'We didn't have a single solitary thing to say to one another' "—and admits to Doris that " 'He sang for me, and it did me good.' " Interestingly, the hymn that Hagar had requested of Mr. Troy is the one " 'that starts out *All people that on earth do dwell*' " (291); thus, the "single solitary" state of alienation and failed speech is pierced by chords addressing all. Song here—as often in the *Vollendungsroman*—seems to leap the gap between silence and speech, bringing into consciousness the individual's yearning for community. It propels Hagar into the kind of recognition which occurs most frequently for the elderly protagonist, a need to shake off the "chains within" and welcome joy.

Words that are delivered to surviving characters, messages that are routed to the dead through intermediaries (so that the elderly character may be delivered from the burden of silence or mistaken speech), talk in which the aged protagonist may exercise a freer version of the self—these are some of the speech acts that point toward affirmation in the *Vollendungsroman*. Always, they are imperfect or imprecise. But that is necessarily the case, since the *Vollendungsroman* negotiates between speech and silence, between the lived and unlived life—and since desire is never satisfied. What seems to matter is that it be expressed.

Hagar's life has been more mistaken than most—her story more unspoken and misspoken—but the distance she feels between what her life has been and what it should have been is entirely typical of the *Vollendungsroman*. I have concocted this German neologism for the novel of old age, of "completion" or "winding up," with a certain measure of irony, since a characteristic of these texts is the recognition that human projects are never completed. Time runs out, as pages do. Only rarely does such a text conclude with a ringing endorsement of what the developmental psychologist Erik Erikson refers to as the old person's "one and only life." An exception of this kind is Willa Cather's "Neighbor Rosicky," which ends with the statement that "Rosicky's life seemed to [the doctor] complete and beautiful"; in Cather's novella, the life itself is regarded as a finished work of art, and closure comes without a pang. But *The Stone Angel*, in which Hagar is struggling desperately to change and grow, in which categorically she refuses to gloss over her mistakes and deprivation, is a far more typical case. Art here reflects *and* seeks to compensate for the incompletion of a human life.

For reasons I shall continue to explore, I would argue that the elderly protagonist has pronounced fictional clout. Simone de Beauvoir, however, in *The Coming of Age*, takes a very different view of the uses of the elderly in fiction: "If an old man is dealt with in his subjective aspect he is not a good hero for a novel; he is finished, set, with no hope, no development to be looked for. . . . Nothing that can happen to him is of any importance" (210). Novels like *The Stone Angel* prove her wrong, resoundingly. But what is particularly striking in this statement is the notion that elderly protagonists cannot engage our interest if "dealt with in [their] subjective aspect." For this is exactly the "aspect" of old age that contemporary fiction chooses to reveal. When the closed subject becomes an open book, when the mask of stereotypical old age is torn away and the icon stirs, when the elderly character in fiction is allowed to reveal herself *as subject*, we discover that indeed there is "development to be looked for." In the case of *The Stone Angel*, that development is "looked for"—by author, character, and reader—all the more urgently because of the constraints that operate against it.

The Stone Angel gives us the elderly protagonist from the inside. A cantankerous old woman, Hagar Shipley is an obstacle and a problem for her family; but we take her side to a remarkable degree, because we are given access to it. (Consider, in contrast, the figure of the "old lady" in Sheila Watson's *The Double Hook*: deprived of access to Mrs. Potter's voice, readers typically accept the desirability of her removal and may even approve her murder.) So we see what Hagar says and does and the effect she has on others—and much of that we would judge harshly; but because Hagar is allowed to tell her own story, because we enter her consciousness and live there, we can respond to her more fairly. We learn to value her rich sensuality and the free play of her wit; we see the other side of the coin, the capacity for joy, all the positive qualities that have been so tragically denied in Hagar's presentation of self to the world. We come to understand as well the social forces—familial, patriarchal, and puritanical—which have led her to this distortion. And that very pride which we deplore in its outer workings, as well as for Hagar's sake, is revealed to us as a means of survival.

The subject of old age is a powerful one for other reasons too. The invisibility or marginalization of old people, their reduction to stereotype, their occupation of a zone behind the mask—all of this may provide special impetus to one of the writer's most crucial drives, which is to *see* other human beings clearly. The indignities suffered by the elderly—as their bodies betray them, as memory fails, as social power is stripped away and condescension mounts—may also stimulate the writer's need to proffer dignity through art. Any reader of *The Stone Angel* will recall how Laurence moves us inexorably (detail by scathing detail) from a puerile assumption of the "we"—" 'Well, how are we today?' he inquires" (277)—to a truer sense of the tribulations of old people.

Questions such as these relate to the elderly person's claim upon a writer's empathy or passion. But the elderly character is also attractive for a number of more 'technical' literary reasons. To begin with, she makes available to the writer nearly the whole span of a life history—as opposed to just that truncated, glibly predictive bit before the heroine decides whom to marry. She picks up the human story at a pivotal and richly dramatic point, when the evaluation of life seems most urgent, and when the old dramatic question of what comes next is most especially poignant. She may also function for the writer as a touchstone (and victim or champion) of social attitudes that have shaped our past and that operate still even in a climate of radical revision. All of this, Hagar clearly does.

The Stone Angel is a prototypical example of the *Vollendungsroman* also in its extensive use of the most characteristic imagery of old age. Consider (for instance) the image of the house, with which Laurence plays so elaborately in using "Stonehouse" as Aunt Doll's surname (to forecast Hagar's tenure as housekeeper in Mr. Oatley's stone house) and in having Marvin sell housepaint (to imply an interest in appearances, which Hagar forswears when she claims the weatherbeaten house at Shadow Point as her own). Laurence begins her manipulation of this image with the old woman's characteristic fear of dispossession. The house is then developed as an image of the self, the societal construct and the body. What Hagar must do in preparation for her death is what Saul Bellow's elderly heroine in "Leaving the Yellow House" and countless others must do. She must wean herself from that cocoon, that carapace of appearances, that entrenched idea of the self, and 'admit' the forces of nature. Understandably, she is afraid. Her fear of intruders in the house is the fear of death that Laurence explores in many strands of the novel's imagery.

Other images that are typical of the *Vollendungsroman* include the sea (which is opposed to the house, as the site of dissolution and rebirth) and the transitional identification of Hagar as a gypsy (who makes her home in nature). Angels—as figures poised between two worlds, as messengers and mediators—are also surprisingly common. The last example I will offer here is the mirror, which Laurence uses (again, typically) in two opposing ways. On the one hand, she holds the mirror up to a literal and appalling truth—as Hagar sees in it "a puffed face purpled with veins as though someone had scribbled over the skin with an indelible pencil" (79)—and on the other hand, she permits Hagar to "feel that if [she] were to walk carefully up to [her] room, approach the mirror softly, take it by surprise, [she] would see there again that Hagar with the shining hair. . . ." (42). In these examples (and others I might have chosen), the power of the image is unleashed by a sense of rich particularity—as if the image had been minted just for Hagar—and by a sense of universality.

Perhaps the most common form of the *Vollendungsroman* is the life review, in which narrative time is divided between past and present. The past—in which the characteristic matter of the *Bildungsroman* is recapitulated—is typically approached and controlled through the operation of the elderly protagonist's memory. The present 'mirrors' the past in a number of complex ways, as the protagonist's most basic identity themes are both reasserted and deconstructed in the final phase of life. Very often—as happens at the point of John's death—the narrative of the past will break off sharply, leaving a gap between that period and the narrative present. At such junctures the possibilities of life appear to close down, the seal of failure is imprinted, and a desirable version of the self seems unattainable. The elderly protagonist will often repress this juncture at which vitality was lost; its eventual approach, however, will be another kind of turning point, a courageous breaking of the seal, releasing her into a new sense of possibility.

If the character's old age is purely a framing device—if little or no attention is paid to development in the present or to the experience of being old—then the novel is not by my definition a *Vollendungsroman*. There are also a number of contemporary novels that focus primarily on the present time of elderly protagonists. Thus, a *Vollendungsroman* like Muriel Spark's *Memento Mori* or Paul Scott's *Staying On* will contain elements of the life review without being structured by this process in the way that *The Stone Angel* clearly is. Generally, however, a considerable portion of the narrative time is spent in the past. In this respect as in many others, Laurence's novel is a kind of template for the genre.

The life review is more than a structural device. It has philosophical implications that take us to the heart of the *Vollendungsroman* and the lives of elderly people. In 1963 (one year prior to the appearance of *The Stone Angel*), Robert N. Butler published an essay called "The Life Review: An Interpretation of Reminiscence in the Aged," in which he posited "the universal occurrence in older people of an inner experience or mental process of reviewing one's life" (65). He was arguing against the custom prevailing at that time, which was "to identify reminiscence in the aged with psychological dysfunction." Butler suggests that "the life review, Janus-like, involves facing death as well as looking back" (67) and that "potentially [it] proceeds towards personality reorganization. Thus, the life review is not synonymous with, but includes reminiscence." It includes also, that is to say, as *The Stone Angel* does, a vital concern with the possibility of change.

Many of Butler's insights and clinical observations are relevant to the case of Hagar, and to the process of the life review as it is depicted in fiction. He remarks, for instance, that "imagery of past events and symbols of death seem frequent in waking life as well as in dreams, suggesting that the life review is a highly visual process" (68). Inherently, then, the life review is a kind of *literary* process as well; and Butler may be cited as supplying evidence for the interpenetration of life and art that helps to characterize the *Vollendungsroman*. The verisimilitude of Hagar's 'poetic' voice, as a register of visually proliferating images—birds and eggs, for example, images that we associate with death and captivity and rebirth—is vindicated by Butler's work.

His essay is also concerned with the question of therapeutic value in the process of the life review. Butler rejects the position of certain psychotherapists that old people should not be encouraged to engage in life review, since they will only be devastated by their failures and their incapacity to repair them. He argues instead for the inherent value of 'truth' and for the possibility of change at any point in the life cycle; he believes, in any case, in the inevitability of the life review. Yet Butler acknowledges the risk for three kinds of people: "those who always tended to avoid the present and put great emphasis on the future. . . . those who have consciously exercised the human capacity to injure others. . . . [and those who are] characterologically arrogant and prideful" (70). Although harsh and incomplete, this might serve a wary therapist as a thumbnail sketch of Hagar Shipley.

Margaret Laurence, however, would not be dissuaded—any more than Hagar is herself. At risk in all these ways, Hagar profits nonetheless (and we profit) from her life review. She "proceeds *toward* personality reorganization" (Butler 67, italics mine). To suggest also how we profit, I shall turn to the work of two other gerontologists. Kathleen Woodward, in her critique of Butler's famous essay, argues that "his notion of plot is Aristotelian; that is, it . . . possesses 'wholeness' . . . and thus unity" (146). Butler is charged with assuming that the life story will be 'resolved' in an out-moded literary way; indeed, in Woodward's view, he *uses* such literature to construct his pleasing, but fallacious, sense of completion in life. But *The Stone Angel* does not actually 'affirm' Hagar's life in terms of unity or wholeness. Indeed, it seizes upon the open ending and upon filaments launched into the future; it discovers hope paradoxically, through the recognition of failure. Certainly it does not ask us to regard Hagar's life as anything like that of Cather's "Neighbor Rosicky."

Laurence in fact directs us toward what Harry R. Moody calls "the public world" (158). First Hagar must go there; dramatically, this is signalled by Hagar's residence in the public ward, where she begins to think of others and to consider the possibility of social change. Thus, she contemplates (for example) a world in which her granddaughter's husband could accept her sturdy independence, a world in which women are acquiring knowledge of their bodies and knowledge that might lead to jobs that use their minds. She gets there, however—to Moody's "public world"—only because she has had the courage to persist in the life review. From that story she learns how other stories might be written *better*.

Moody's idea is that the story should be told out loud. The life review process should transport the elderly person from a private and solipsistic space into a public one, in which the story can be heard. Thus, Moody is concerned less with the therapeutic value of the life review than with its importance for society at large; his interest is focussed on the loss to society that is entailed by our narcissistic denial of the experience of the aged. Reminiscence, Moody suggests, is not—as Aristotle thought—opposed to hope: "It is the other way around" (160), since " 'old people live and remember for the sake of the future' " (161). But Moody recognizes as well the benefit that accrues to the old person whose story is heard: "The singing of the song and the telling of the tale *must* become public in order to shine through the natural ruin of time."

The public story is never finished. And neither is the private one, though it needs to be told (however partially) before the story is cut off: "And then—" It needs telling for its contribution to the public story, and because the elderly person must know that the communal realm is somehow real, if she is not to feel that her annihilation is complete. She can stand—Hagar can—the knowledge that "the plagues go on from generation to generation" (284) and that "nothing is ever changed at a single stroke" (88); she can stand to know (and *needs* to know) that her own life has been a failure, in most of the ways that count. But she needs to speak. Hagar has only begun to speak "the heart's truth" when her time runs out; and she has little chance to review her life for others, although she makes a crucial start with Murray Lees.

Happily—for Hagar's sake, I'd like to say, as well as for ours—her insistent voice was heard in the "Shadow Point" of Margaret Laurence's subconscious. There it grew, by nature and by art. It became at last the "forest" of Laurence's text, where the voice of Hagar Shipley speaks. It became "a forest, through which one can see outward, in which the shapes of trees do not prevent air and sun, and in which the trees themselves are growing structures, something alive." And it became that through the force of Margaret Laurence's compassionate imagination. . . . I knew Margaret Laurence only slightly—I spent no more than a dozen hours in her company—but I think I learned this much: that Laurence was moved above all by the need to fight, for herself and others, a need to lend her womanly strength. She had a lot of Hagar in her—and as Hagar would have wished she wrote *with her own life* a better story.

Works Consulted

Butler, Robert N. "The Life Review: An Interpretation of Reminiscence in the Aged." *Psychiatry* 26.1 (1963): 65-76.

de Beauvoir, Simone. *The Coming of Age*. New York: Putnam's, 1972.

Laurence, Margaret. "Gadgetry or Growing: Form and Voice in the Novel." *Journal of Canadian Fiction* 27.1 (1980): 54-62.

_________. *The Stone Angel*. Toronto: McClelland and Stewart, New Canadian Library, 1982.

Moody, Harry R. "Reminiscence and the Recovery of the Public World." *Journal of Gerontological Social Work* 7.1/2 (1984): 157-66.

New, W.H. "Every Now and Then: Voice and Language in Laurence's *The Stone Angel*." *Canadian Literature* 93 (1982): 79-96.

Woodward, Kathleen. "Reminiscence and the Life Review: Prospects and Retrospects." *What Does It Mean to Grow Old?: Reflections from the Humanities*. Ed. Thomas R. Cole and Sally Gadow. Durham, N.C.: Duke University Press, 1986. 135-61.

Paul Hjartarson
University of Alberta

"Christie's Real Country. Where I Was Born": Story-Telling, Loss and Subjectivity in *The Diviners*

We are forever telling stories about ourselves.
—Roy Schafer

I

*T*HE DIVINERS OPENS with a contradiction, "an apparently impossible contradiction": "The river," the narrator declares, "flowed both ways" (3). Although this apparent contradiction is immediately explained as an optical illusion, the image lingers in the mind. It lingers because in the opening pages of *The Diviners* the river becomes a figure for the dynamic and apparently contradictory process by which the protagonist of the novel, the forty-seven-year-old writer, Morag Gunn, appears, on the one hand, to shape and give meaning to the life story she tells and, on the other, to be entirely shaped, to be herself composed by the stories told. The river that flows both ways becomes, that is, a figure for the fascinating process by which Morag both designates herself and is designated as a speaking subject, speaks herself and is spoken as a woman situated aslant the patriarchal discourses of her day. This apparently contradictory process holds our attention as much as the river does Morag; the river we watch, however, does not flow by Morag's log cabin. Our river takes its name from the opening section of the novel; it is the "River of Now and Then," a river less of time than of narrative; it is, in particular, *the* narrative, the NOW and THEN, of *The Diviners* itself. The "apparently impossible contradiction" we witness is that, unlike Morag's river, time and narrative do indeed flow both ways, that we shape our past, and hence our selves, as much as the past shapes us. "*A popular misconception*," Morag reflects early in the novel, "*is that we can't change the past*," but, she asserts, "*—everyone is constantly changing their own past, recalling it, revising it*" (60). *The Diviners* is written, in part, against that popular misconception.

Unfortunately, that misconception has, for the most part, informed the reception of Laurence's novel. Faced with the "apparently impossible contradiction," readers have concluded that rivers, after all, flow just one way. David Staines' comment in his Introduction to the New Canadian Library edition of *The Diviners* is representative of reader response to the novel generally. "The central lesson of the novel and of Morag's self-exploration," he writes, is "the inability to escape the past" (viii). That reading tells only half the story: it acknowledges the importance of the past in determining Morag's present life but it ignores the role of the present in shaping Morag's understanding of her past. What is more, it assumes that Morag's past is not only inescapable but immutable. Morag knows better—for she has learned that the past and, with it, self-knowledge is the story we tell.

The life of a writer, and hence a novel in the tradition of the *künstlerroman*, *The Diviners* is the story of a story-teller, a story about story-telling that is itself composed of stories. It consists, however, of two main narratives: the story of NOW, that is, of Morag's life as a forty-seven-year-old writer and single parent; and the story of THEN, that is, of Morag's past. Although the narrative of Morag's past is embedded in and subordinate to the story of her present life, most commentaries focus on that past and conceive the novel as the story of Morag's rejection and subsequent acceptance of Manawaka and of her life as the garbage collector's daughter. Such a reading moves from the youthful Morag's fierce denial to Jules that Christie is her father—"Christie's not my old man. My dad is dead" (72)—to the older woman's acceptance of her Manawaka parentage: "I used to fight a lot with you, Christie," she declares to him on his deathbed, "but you've been my father to me" (396). It moves, too, from her rejection of his stories as "a load of old manure" (162) to her affirmation of the need for and value of such story-telling (418). That affirmation is implicit not only in the tales of Christie, Lazarus and others with which Morag entertains Pique, but in the novels the older woman publishes. All these events are recounted; all the stories told; all Morag's novels summarized in the THEN of the novel.

In this reading, the NOW narrative provides little more than a point of view on the past. In "Laurence and the Use of Memory" Leona Gom articulates this position clearly. Arguing that *The Diviners* presents the reader with two Morags, Gom declares that "there is less reader interest in the older Morag" than in the younger woman:

> The older Morag, unsure as she may be as to the best way to handle situations, particularly with Pique, is nevertheless a self-aware character, and probably more secure in her identity than are any of Laurence's heroines. The reader thus is rarely able to see more than Morag herself does, and the woman that is introduced at the first of the book is not significantly different from the woman at the end. . . . Morag grows and learns, particularly in her relationship with Christie, throughout the second narrative level, but does not

> move toward a significant character development on the first level; she has, in a way . . . already 'arrived' when the novel begins. (56)

According to Gom, our attention is focussed on the narrative of Morag's past because the NOW of the novel offers us little more than a destination; in *The Diviners* we watch the child grow into the woman we meet at the outset of the novel.

The problem with Gom's argument, and with this reading of *The Diviners*, is that our attention in the NOW narrative centres not on Morag's character development, not on change through time, but on the *process* by which Morag composes herself in the stories she tells, by which, in the *act* of story-telling, she gives meaning and shape to the events in her life. In "River of Now and Then" we witness Morag in the act of interpreting herself to herself through the stories she tells; what is more, we are made aware that this activity has been a life-long process. "*I recall looking at the pictures*," she says of some childhood photographs, "*these pictures, over and over again, each time imagining I remembered a little more*" (9). This activity, in the NOW narrative, changes Morag so that, contrary to what Gom suggests, the woman who parts with her daughter at the end of *The Diviners* is not the woman we are introduced to at the beginning.

To privilege the narrative of Morag's past, to view Morag in terms of that "inescapable past," is to conceive her largely as a product of that past. To privilege the NOW narrative is to view Morag in terms of her present life, to conceive her in the process of understanding herself. The one views self as product; the other, as process. Laurence insists on both. "The river flow[s] both ways." Past events in *The Diviners* are narrated in the present tense; present events, in the past tense. What is more, Laurence offers us two perspectives on her protagonist. We see Morag from the inside; we share her thoughts, experience her feelings; we witness her coming to terms with her life; we see her in the act of writing, of giving significant shape to that life. At the same time, Laurence's use of the third person forces us to view Morag from the outside, from a distance; we see her shaped by her experiences; we see her not composing her life-story but composed by it, a product of the forces acting on her and subject to the patriarchal discourses of her day.

II

The opening section of *The Diviners*, "River of Now and Then," centres on two experiences of loss. The first concerns Morag's relation to her eighteen-year-old daughter, Pique. *The Diviners* opens on the morning Morag awakens to find that her only child has left home. "Pique had gone away. She must have left during the night" (3). That loss prompts Morag to dig out some "photographs from the past" and, in looking at them, to recall her childhood. She makes it very clear, however, that the photographs occasion rather than in themselves contain these childhood memories. "*I keep these snapshots not for what they show but for what is hidden in them*" (6). The memories, we quickly realize, are "hidden" not in the photographs but in Morag's mind; what is more, Morag herself acknowledges that her "memories" are "invented," that is, that they are stories she began composing as a child. "*All this is crazy, of course*," she declares about the memories she associates with the second snapshot: "*and quite untrue. Or maybe true and maybe not. I am remembering myself composing this interpretation, in Christie and Prin's house*" (8). Concerning her commentary on the following snapshot she reflects:

> *I don't recall when I invented that one. I can remember it, though, very clearly. Looking at the picture and knowing what was hidden in it. I must've made it up much later on, long long after something terrible happened.* (9)

The effect of these thoughts is to foreground not the memory itself but the act of composition, the process by which, over the years, Morag has articulated her past and conceived herself through story. In the opening pages of the novel, we witness Morag less in the act of recalling her past than in the process of composing it; what is more, we are made aware that she has been engaged in that activity since childhood.

The second experience of loss is occasioned by the first. The loss Morag feels at Pique's unexpected and unannounced departure leads her to recall and, in recalling, to relive the most traumatic loss she has suffered, the death of her parents when she was a child. Whereas the memories she associates with the snapshots are "*totally invented*" (10), the death of her parents, she notes, is "*somewhat ironically . . . the first memory* [she] *can trust.*" But, then, she adds:

> *I can't trust it completely, either, partly because I recognize anomalies in it, ways of expressing the remembering, ways which aren't those of a five-year-old, as though I were older in that memory (and the words bigger) than in some subsequent ones when I was six or seven, and partly because it was only what was happening to Me. What was happening to everyone else? What really happened in the upstairs bedroom?* (13)

Unlike the earlier stories, Morag's account of her parents' death is presented not as a commentary on a snapshot but as a "Memorybank Movie," the first such "movie" in the novel. To underline its fictional nature, to emphasize that it *is* a story and not a transcription from life, the Memorybank Movie is titled "Once Upon a Time There Was."

Although Morag acknowledges that her memory of her parents' death is a story she has composed, as much fiction as fact, her recollection of it moves her to tears. "*Now I am crying, for God's sake*" she declares in exasperation, "*and I don't even know how much of that memory really happened and how much of it I embroidered later on*" (17-18). Finally, however, Morag acknowledges that her questions about what "really happened" are "meaningless" because she recognizes that the past and with it, subjectivity, is inaccessible other than as narrative, as a story we tell. "*What really happened?*" she asks later, "*A meaningless question. But one I keep trying to answer, knowing there is no answer*" (60). Those attempts are made through story.

The Diviners, like all *künstlerromans*—indeed, like all (fictional) autobiographies—involves a search for origins. In *The Diviners* Laurence locates the self in story and the need to tell stories in the experience of loss. "Hearing the silence of the world, the failure of the world to announce meaning," Robert Kroetsch writes, "we tell stories" (83). In *The Diviners* Laurence appears to predicate our need to tell stories on a similar feeling of silence, of loss. All the stories recounted in the opening section of the novel date from "*after something terrible happened*," that is, from the death of Morag's parents. All seem intended to fill the void left by the loss of her parents. "*I can't remember myself actually composing them*," Morag states concerning these memories of her parents, "*but it must have happened so*" (11).

> *How much later? At Christie's, of course, putting myself to sleep. I cannot really remember my parents' faces at all. When I look now at that one snapshot of them, they aren't faces I can relate to anyone I ever knew. It didn't bother me for years and years. Why should it grieve me now? Why do I want them back? What could my mother and I say to one another? I'm more than ten years older now than she was when she died—and she would seem so young to me, so inexperienced.* (11)

But she does grieve—both for her absent daughter and for her dead parents—and, like her younger self, she tells stories against the silence, against the loss: "Once Upon a Time There Was."

In "River of Now and Then" the forty-seven-year-old recalls the few memories she has of her early childhood and once again grieves over the death of her parents. *"They remain shadows,"* she laments,

> *Two sepia shadows on an old snapshot, two barely moving shadows in my head, shadows whose few remaining words and acts I have invented. Perhaps I only want their forgiveness for having forgotten them.*
>
> *I remember their death, but not their lives. Yet they're inside me, flowing unknown in my blood and moving unrecognized in my skull.* (18-19)

The language here is of privation, of what is "unknown," "unrecognized," lost. Although Morag remembers her parents' deaths and not their lives, although they remain "sepia shadows," they inhabit her and shape her existence. They exist as characters in the stories the older Morag tells herself, much as the child did, to deny the absence, to overcome the loss, to people the silence; and these stories structure her life, as they did that of her younger self, and determine who she is.

Nowhere is the relation of story-telling, loss and subjectivity made more apparent than in the account, in the THEN narrative, of how Christie comes to tell Morag his "First Tale of Piper Gunn." That account, itself retrospective, is contained in a Memorybank Movie titled "Christie with Spirits." Christie has been drinking, and when "the spirits start to get gloomy in him," nine-year-old Morag asks him for a story about Piper Gunn.

> Christie sighs and pours another drink. He sits there, thinking. Soon he will begin. Morag knows what it says in the book [*The Clans and Tartans of Scotland*] under the name Gunn. It isn't fair but it must be true because it is right there in the book:

> The chieftainship of Clan Gunn is undetermined at the present time and no arms have been matriculated.
>
> When she first looked it up, she showed it to Christie, and he read it and then he laughed and asked her if she had not been told the tales about the most famous Gunn of all, and so he told her. He tells them to her sometimes when the spirit moves him.
>
> Now he rocks back on the straight chair, for he is sitting at the table with the bottle beside him.
>
> "All right, then, listen and I will tell you the first tale of your ancestor." (48)

Bereft of parents, Morag is also denied an ancestry, denied a place in the discourse of the past. Christie tells Morag the tales of her ancestors, of Piper Gunn "and his woman Morag," to open a space for her, to situate her in that discourse. In bed later, Morag tells *herself* the "Tale of Piper Gunn's Woman." Having listened to Christie's stories, having heard herself named, Morag can, in turn, name herself, insert herself in story, become herself the teller: "Once long ago there was a beautiful woman name of Morag . . ." (52). The story-telling empowers Morag both as a woman and as a speaking subject. "*I have the power*," the Morag in her tale declares, "*and the second sight and the good eye and the strength of conviction*" (52).

Morag's later rejection, in the THEN narrative, of her step-parents and of Manawaka is, at the same time, a denial of this story-telling and of herself as a speaking subject. If Christie and his story-telling are the focus of "The Nuisance Grounds" section of the novel, then Morag's stepmother, Prin—short for princess—is the centre of "The Halls of Sion" section and she is a figure for silence, for women written by the discourse of patriarchal narratives. The section takes its title from Prin's favourite hymn, and singing that hymn—about "the halls of Sion" forever occupied by "the Prince"—at

Prin's funeral leads Morag to question the implied narrative of her marriage to Brooke and her own role as "princess."

> Those halls of Sion. The Prince is ever in them. What has Morag expected, those years ago, marrying Brooke? Those selfsame halls?
>
> And now here, in this place, the woman who brought Morag up is lying dead, and Morag's mind, her attention, has left Prin. *Help me, God; I'm frightened of myself.* (253)

It is shortly after Prin's funeral that Morag truly begins to stand up to Brooke, to find her own voice (256), and to feel confident in her own abilities as a novelist (260).

III

Readers who argue that *The Diviners* is concerned with Morag's "inability to escape the past" tend to focus attention on two related conversations. The first occurs in the THEN of the novel when Morag is a university student in Winnipeg. Having accepted her English professor's offer of marriage and preparing to move to Toronto, she returns to Manawaka for a brief visit. Drinking whiskey with Christie in the kitchen, she apologizes for not inviting him to her wedding. "Look here," he declares, "it's a bloody good thing you've got away from this dump. So just shut your goddamn trap and thank your lucky stars." Surprised by his response, Morag asks:

> "Do you really think that, Chistie?"
>
> "I do," Christie says, knocking back the whiskey. "And also I don't. That's the way it goes. It'll all go along with you, too. That goes without saying."
>
> But it has been said. *The way it goes—it'll all go—that goes*. Does Christie bring in these echoes knowingly, or does it just happen naturally with him? She has never known.
>
> "You mean—everything will go along with me?"

"No less than that, ever," Christie says.

"It won't, though," Morag says, and hears the stubbornness in her own voice.

"Who says so, Morag?"

"I say so." (207)

Morag is here caught in one of many apparent contradictions, for even as she denies Christie's assertion that "it'll all go along with [her]," she recognizes in his speech echoes, arguably unconscious echoes, of the past. Seeking desperately to escape Manawaka and the life narrative it appears to offer, she marries her "Prince Charming," and thus truly becomes Prin's daughter. Seeking to escape, to silence her past, Morag cannot, at this point in her life, accept either Christie's way of speaking or his simple truth.

Years later, Morag not only discovers echoes of Christie's speech in her own but recognizes the wisdom in his words: "Christie knew things about inner truths," the older woman writes her friend, Ella, "that I am only just beginning to understand" (418). What is more, in the NOW of *The Diviners* she attempts to offer that wisdom to another, her daughter's boyfriend, Dan Scranton, who is seeking to escape his own past as the son of a wealthy ranching family. "They think I'm some kind of traitor," he declares of his parents, "—to them, to everything."

> "But I'm not going back to take over the place from him, not even when he's dead. I don't want his kind of place. Not in any way."
>
> "Yet you're planning to raise horses," Morag ventured.
>
> Morag Gunn, fleeing Manawaka, finally settling near McConnell's Landing, an equally small town with many of the same characteristics.
>
> "That's different," Dan said defensively. "I have to make my own kind of place. I'm not talking about the difference in outside scenery, either."

> "I know. Your own place will be different, but it'll be the same, too, in some ways."
>
> "Not if I can help it," Dan said angrily.
>
> "I'm not sure you *can* help it. You can change a whole lot. But you can't throw him away entirely. He and a lot of others are there. Here."
>
> Morag reached out and touched the vein on Dan's wrist. (354)

The older woman knows what her younger self did not, that—as Morag states paragraphs later—"Islands are unreal," that "No place is far enough away" (356). Morag recognizes, in short, that the self is not an island, "not an essence, but a set of relationships" (Silverman 52). She realizes that "No place is far enough away" because those relationships exist as much within us as without, so that while Dan is able to leave home he cannot escape the relationships that people his mind and guide his actions. "You can change a whole lot," she tells him, "But you can't throw him away entirely. He and a lot of others are there. Here" (*Div* 356).

This view could lead to a simple determinism, a cult of the past, of the blood: you are your past, you are what the past has made of you. Dan's salvation, however, like Morag's, lies in the fact that the past is held in the mind as image, as story. The past may be inescapable but, as story, it is not immutable. "*Everyone*," Morag affirms, "*is constantly changing their own past, recalling it, revising it*" (60).

Among the many stories embedded in *The Diviners* are the accounts of the four novels Morag has published, *Spears of Innocence, Prospero's Child, Jonah, Shadows of Eden*, and a book of short stories titled *Presences*. As Ildikó de Papp Carrington has noted, these published stories all bear some relation to events in Morag's personal life. In them, Morag reconceives and rewrites her past and her self. *Jonah*, her third novel, for example, is a re-vision of her relationship with Christie.

> [It] is the story of an old man, a widower, who is fairly disreputable and who owns a gillnetter in Vancouver. He fishes the mouth of the Fraser River and the Strait of Georgia when the salmon run is on. It is also about his daughter Coral, who resents his not being a reputable character. Jonah inhabits Morag's head, and talks in his own voice. In some ways she knows more about Coral, who is so uncertainly freed by Jonah's ultimate death, but it is Jonah himself who seems more likely to take on his own life in the fiction. (366)

As Papp Carrington points out, this summary of the novel is immediately followed by "Morag's Tale of Christie Logan" (366-67), the story of Morag's initial rejection and later acceptance of her garbage-collecting stepfather and of the stories he told. Both lead directly to Morag's subsequent acknowledgement not only that Christie has been a father to her but that her life has been shaped, her self formed, by the stories he told her.

In the concluding paragraph of *The Diviners* Morag "return[s] to the house, to write the remaining private and fictional words, and to set down her title" (453). If, as Leona Gom (51-52), Ildikó de Papp Carrington (154) and others have argued, the THEN narrative of *The Diviners* is the novel on which Morag is currently working, then her fifth book is more openly and directly autobiographical than her earlier books, for its protagonist is a character named not Lilac, Miranda, or Coral, but Morag. All the novels, however, are autobiographical in that each, like *The Diviners*, involves divining for the self. That self exists not as an essence, not as something Morag can find—as Royland finds water—but as stories she tells, stories she composes but which also compose her.

Nowhere is this made more apparent than in Morag's decision not to visit Sutherland, "where her people came from" (369). She makes that decision while visiting her lover,

Dan McRaith, and his wife in Scotland. Walking with Morag, "McRaith points across the firth, to the north."

> "Away over there is Sutherland, Morag Dhu, where your people came from. When do you want to drive there?"
>
> Morag considers.
>
> "I thought I would have to go. But I guess I don't, after all."
>
> "Why would that be?"
>
> "I don't know that I can explain. It has to do with Christie. The myths are my reality. Something like that. And also, I don't need to go there because I know now what it was I had to learn here."
>
> "What is that?"
>
> "It's a deep land here, all right," Morag says. "But it's not mine, except a long long way back. I always thought it was the land of my ancestors, but it is not."
>
> "What is, then?"
>
> "Christie's real country. Where I was born." (390-91)

With these words Morag locates her past, locates her self, in the world of stories, "Christie's real world. Where I was born." "The myths" *are* her "reality": they structure her life; they are the means by which she designates herself and is designated as a subject.

IV

In *Mother and Daughter Relationships in the Manawaka World of Margaret Laurence*, Helen Buss argues that the tone of the second section of *The Diviners*, "The Nuisance Grounds," "is one of denigration and shame" (68). That sense of denigration and shame informs not just "The Nuisance Grounds" but the whole THEN narrative. Whereas the second section of the novel is concerned with the shame and denigration Morag feels as the scavenger's daughter, the third, "The Halls of Sion," centres on the denigration and shame she feels as Mrs. Brooke Skelton, a self written by the patriarchal discourse, a self without a past and without a voice. Morag discovers both in the act of writing *Spears of Innocence*. "Rites of Passage," the third section of the novel and the final section of the THEN narrative, focusses on Morag's realization of herself as a writer and as a mother through the novels she publishes and through the stories she tells both herself and her daughter. "Rite of passage" here involves not just an initiation, Morag's discovery of herself, but her composition of that self *through story*, her passage through narrative, a passage that enables her to situate herself as a speaking subject aslant the patriarchal discourses of her day.

That narrative, however, is embedded in the story of Morag's present life and the primary concern of the NOW narrative, as Buss herself recognizes, is the experience of loss. The concluding section of *The Diviners*, itself titled "The Diviners," is set entirely in the NOW of the novel. In it, we see Morag coming to terms with loss. That process is evident throughout the NOW narrative; however, "The Diviners" juxtaposes moments of loss Morag has experienced up to that point in her life with three new losses: the loss of Pique, who announces that she is moving west; the loss of Jules, whose death occurs at this point in the novel; and the possible loss of her own powers as a diviner.

In the opening pages of "The Diviners" Pique finally offers her mother an account of the trip to Manawaka, an account she has withheld up to now for fear of upsetting her mother. Pique has reason to be concerned for her narrative evokes many of the losses Morag experienced in Manawaka. It begins in the valley with Pique's visit to the Tonnerre shack, where Morag first experienced sexual intercourse and where Piquette and her children died in the fire that consumed the old shack; it ends with Pique's ascent to the Manawaka cemetery to find Christie and Prin's grave. There Pique meets Eva Winkler—"*Well, now, think of that; I'm glad Morag did have a child after all*" (438)—whose aborted foetus Christie buried in the Nuisance Grounds. Pique's account ends there because Morag is in tears.

> "Ma—I did upset you, didn't I? I'm sorry. You're crying."
>
> "It's okay. Honestly. It's just—well, I guess I can't explain."
>
> Too many years. No brief summary possible. Accept it and let it go. (438)

But there is more to come. Pique announces that she is "going west again" (438), and that announcement is followed almost immediately by news from Billy Joe that Jules is dying.

The narrative of Morag's visit to her dying lover, Pique's father, is the central event of "The Diviners," central not simply because it is placed between the other two experiences of loss in this section but because it recalls and enables Morag to re-conceive and complete the earlier narrative of her own parents' death when she was a child. Morag's profound feeling of loss stems, in part, from the fact that she is barred from seeing her dying parents. "I want to see my mother," five-year-old Morag demands.

> "I am going up to see her right now. I won't stay long, Mrs. Pearl. I promise."
>
> But the Big Person grabs Morag's wrist before Morag can slither away. Mrs. Pearl's hands are very strong, a trap like for mice or gophers or that, crunching down.
>
> "No, you don't," Mrs. Pearl says sharply. "They're too sick to see you, just now, Morag. They don't want to see you."
>
> "How do you know?" Morag cries. "You don't know anything about it! They do *so*! Let go of me!" (14-15)

But, finally, it is her own fear that the five-year-old must overcome. Mrs. Pearl has Morag sleep in the kitchen and keeps the door locked at night "so that Morag will not wander upstairs" (14). One night, however, Mrs. Pearl forgets to lock the door.

> Dr. MacLeod had been that evening, and Morag had been sent out to play long after supper, when it was nearly dark. Mrs. Pearl's face looked scary when she put Morag to bed, but she said not a word.
>
> Morag is alone in the dark. The stove hisses a little, and sighs, as the fire dies down. Morag gets up and tries the door and it opens into the livingroom. She stands barefoot, the linoleum cool on her skin, and listens.
>
> From upstairs, there is a sound. Crying. Crying? Yes, crying. Not like people, though. Like something else. She does not know what. Kiy-oots. She knows only that it is her father's voice. There is no sound of her mother's voice, no sound at all.
>
> Morag, terrified, scuttles back to the kitchen like a cockroach—she *is* a cockroach; she feels like one, running, scuttling. (15-16).

Morag is terrified both by the silence—"There is no sound of her mother's voice, no sound at all"—and by the sound of her father crying, grieving over the loss of his wife and in the knowledge of his own impending death. Although Morag recognizes the voice as her father's, the sound seems inhuman, the sound of a "kiy-oot," lost like the five-year-old in a world of fear and death.

In the narrative of Jules' death, the five-year-old, now forty-seven, in effect, climbs the stairs and opens the door to the bedroom.

> Outside the door to Jules' room, Billy Joe stopped. He looked oddly determined, as though Jules might not approve of what he had done, but also as though he knew that this was necessary and what Jules wanted even though in an unadmitted way.
>
> Then he left her, and went into his own room. Now Morag was afraid. Not afraid, any longer, that Jules

> might mock her or tell her to get out. Not that, not now. Simply afraid of what she might see, of how he might look. Afraid that she might have to look at something she could not bear to look at. She opened the door. (443)

Morag fears, in short, to look on the face of death. She not only overcomes that fear but is able to comfort, and to be comforted by, her dying lover:

> The night was wearing on. Finally Morag got up and turned out the light. Kicked off her shoes and lay down beside him, both of them clad, lying silently, connected only by their hands.
>
> Then Jules turned to her and put his arms around her, and she put her arms around him. The brief sound in the darkness was the sound of a man crying the knowledge of his death. (446-47)

Whereas the five-year-old feels both locked out and locked in, frighteningly alone, the forty-seven-year-old lives in the knowledge not only of death but of comfort given and received.

She lives, too, with the knowledge that she has kept Jules' dying from Pique. "*How can I not tell her about Jules' death? How can I tell her*?" she agonizes:

> *He doesn't want me to tell her. He doesn't want to see her. He wants to see her, but not for her to see him.*
>
> The aeons ago memory. The child saying *I'll just go up and see my mother and father, now, for a minute.* And Mrs. Pearl, holding tightly to the child's wrist, saying *No you don't; they're too sick to see you; they don't want to.* They had wanted to see her; they had not wanted her to see them. The gaps in understanding, the long-ago child wondering what was being kept from her, wondering why they did not want to see her. Morag had been five. Pique was not a child. Nevertheless, she would want to see him and would not likely understand why she must not. (447)

Thus the older woman rewrites the earlier narrative, filling in the gaps in understanding: "They had wanted to see her; they had not wanted her to see them."

She is now both the child and the "Big Person"; however, she is able—as Mrs. Pearl was apparently not—to mediate between her child and the dying parent. She gives the words of Pique's song to Jules, and his knife, to her. What is more, she is able to comfort, and to be comforted by, her daughter.

> Morag phoned to A-Okay's and told Maudie to ask Pique to come over. Morag had not cried. When Pique arrived, she saw the knife on the table.
>
> "Ma—something's happened to him, hasn't it?"
>
> "Yes. He's dead. Of throat cancer."
>
> Abruptly, like that. Unable to speak it otherwise. Pique said nothing. Then crumpled, knelt, put her head on Morag's lap and cried. But later, when she rose and saw her mother's face, it was she who comforted Morag. (448-49)

Morag cannot bring herself to tell Pique the full story—that Jules committed suicide rather than continue to suffer through the illness. The "gaps in understanding" are still there—we are led to believe that they are always there—but there is consolation.

In *Mother and Daughter Relationships* Helen Buss notes that Pique's second leave-taking is much more "open and loving" than her earlier "middle-of-the-night runaway" (73). It is more positive, in part, because Morag has come to terms with her own feelings of loss and loneliness and is therefore better able to send her daughter off on the necessary pilgrimage. When Pique asks, "Ma— . . . you'll take care, eh? You'll be okay?" Morag answers without hesitation, "Of course. I *am* okay," to which the narrative voice adds, "And in a profound sense, this was true" (450).

Morag is thus finally able to understand what she has always sensed she might learn from Royland; indeed, she realizes that she has "known it all along, but not really known." Royland arrives at Morag's door to announce that he has lost the gift of divining, but he has also come to tell her that "the gift" may well have been given to A-Okay and "that quite a few people can learn to do it."

> The inheritors. Was this, finally and at last, what Morag had always sensed she had to learn from the old man? She had known it all along, but not really known. The gift, or portion of grace, or whatever it was, was finally withdrawn, to be given to someone else.
>
> "This that's happened to me—" Royland said, "it's not a matter for mourning."
>
> "I see that now," Morag said. (452)

Like the earlier exchanges with Pique and with Jules—not to mention with Christie—this exchange is an affirmation of community, of humanity. Morag has gone from conceiving herself as an island to realizing herself in relationships, and in so doing, she lives not only with the knowledge of loss but with the recognition of inheritance, of community.

When Royland declares that what has happened to him is "not a matter of mourning," Morag utters the final words spoken in the novel: "I see that now." These words lead her to the river and to the vision that enables her to complete the novel she is writing: "*Look ahead into the past, and back into the future, until the silence.*" Morag's story-telling is an act of faith undertaken not only in the knowledge of that silence but in an affirmation of community, and in that affirmation she finds her title: the diviners, not one, but a community of them, realizing themselves not in isolation but in their relations with others both past and present.

V

In this reading of *The Diviners* I have privileged the NOW narrative; what is more, I have ignored—among other things—the novel's relation to other texts in the Manawaka series. I have, in effect, written again the prevailing current of Laurence criticism which both privileges the THEN narrative and reads *The Diviners* almost entirely in light of the earlier novels. My purpose is not to deny the importance either of the THEN narrative or of *The Diviners*' relation to the earlier texts. I suspect that our understanding of *The Diviners* develops out of our sense of the relation between the two narrative levels, between the NOW and the THEN. Given that the THEN narrative is embedded in and subordinate to the NOW, and that most readings have privileged the story of Morag's past, I have written with the desire to redress, in some small measure, the imbalance, and to affirm with Laurence's narrator that the river, the river of NOW and THEN, "flow[s] both ways."

Works Consulted

Bailey, Nancy. "Fiction and the New Androgyne: Problems and Possibilities in *The Diviners*." *Atlantis* 4.1 (1978): 10-17.

Bennett, Donna A. "The Failure of Sisterhood in Margaret Laurence's Novels." *Atlantis* 4.1 (1978): 103-09.

Buss, Helen M. *Mother and Daughter Relationships in the Manawaka Works of Margaret Laurence*. The ELS Monograph Series. Victoria: University of Victoria Press, 1985.

Gom, Leona M. "Laurence and the Use of Memory." *Canadian Literature* 71 (1976): 48-58.

Howells, Coral Ann. *Private and Fictional Words: Canadian Woman Novelists of the 1970s and 1980s*. London: Methuen, 1987.

Kroetsch, Robert. "Beyond Nationalism: A Prologue." *Robert Kroetsch: Essays. Open Letter* 5th ser. 4 (1983): 83-89.

Laurence, Margaret. *The Diviners*. 1974. Toronto: Bantam-Seal, 1975.

Maeser, Angelika. "Finding the Mother: The Individuation of

Laurence's Heroines." *Journal of Canadian Fiction* 27 (1980): 151-66.

Papp Carrington, Ildikó de. " 'Tales in the Telling': *The Diviners* as Fiction about Fiction." *Essays on Canadian Writing* 9 (1977-78): 1-14.

Schafer, Roy. "Narration in the Psychoanalytic Dialogue." *Critical Inquiry* 7.1 (1980): 29-53.

Silverman, Kaja. *The Subject of Semiotics*. New York: Oxford U.P., 1983.

Staines, David. Introduction. *The Diviners*. New Canadian Library No. 146. Toronto: McClelland and Stewart, 1978.

Craig Tapping
University of British Columbia

Margaret Laurence and Africa

To begin, I would like to recount one of my own experiences as a new professor at a university in eastern Nigeria at the end of 1979. I remember walking into my first class, and being somewhat hesitant about my position and authority as I looked about me and remarked on several young people dressed as spectacularly as any you might expect to meet at one of the so-called developed world's more sophisticated night clubs. They were so hip, and I was so foreign. And, to break the ice, I began like I have begun here: with an introduction about my life and studies, and about previous teaching assignments I had had. Imagine my surprise when, after explaining that I had studied for my B.A. in Vancouver, the class boomed out in unison, "Canada!" My previous experiences in attempting to locate my youth geographically had all occurred in Europe during the 1970s, and usually produced dismal misunderstandings! If I was lucky, and someone did recognize that I had come from a country with a political and cultural identity quite distinct from that of the United States, there were still quite remarkable hurdles to overcome in my experience of European condescension as it masked ignorance of an outside world. Once, for example, I was actually reading a novel by Margaret Laurence—*The Fire-Dwellers*, I think it was—when a colleague at an English university asked me, in all seriousness, "Do they have a literature in Canada yet?"

And so here I was, thirty miles upriver from Conrad's Little Popo where Marlow had stopped for fuel and provisions before journeying on into what Europeans have traditionally regarded as the heart of their darkness, in a class of perhaps eighty African first-year Arts students, and all of them were shouting "Canada" at me or cheering with unabashed abandonment. As I smiled and blushed, and order was restored, my confusion demanded some explanations. "Why do you all get so excited about Canada?" I asked. It was the late seventies, and even Canadians—according to what I could gather from the CBC World Service—were excited about the place, but I had been away from Canada for over a decade, and had therefore missed out on this new pride.

Some students whom I had already encountered under the shade trees outside began to explain that every Nigerian wanted to be a writer because writers brought dignity and culture to their society. I was still puzzled. One student, however, persisted above the din: one Canadian had done more than any other person to promote Nigerian writing internationally and, in so doing, had examined the crucial role writers play in building a culture. And that Canadian was Margaret Laurence, in her book *Long Drums and Cannons*.

And so, it is a double privilege for me to write about Margaret Laurence and about the newly published literatures and ancient oral systems which she encountered in Africa. I will attempt to explain what these narrative traditions taught her about her own writing, and hope that I can convey my sense of how this perception of an entirely different culture, which nonetheless shares a fundamentally common history with her own, shaped Margaret Laurence's understanding of Canadian writing as one of a family: the new literatures in English which have emerged since mid-century.

In order to give some shape to what I wish to say, I think it easiest to imagine Margaret Laurence's Africa as a varied and multi-faceted subject. And the most immediate and obvious distinction is that between her African criticism and her African fictions. And, although the criticism actually predates her creative writing, it should also be read as the apprentice-work to those fictions. In other words, there is no abrupt and sudden change, but rather the gradual empowering of a personal voice which would come back to Canada and do, in her writings, what those voices she discusses in her criticism of African traditions do, and had done, for their cultures and peoples.

Although an apparent confusion may exist in the chronology of publication, Laurence clearly asserts that the criticism came first. Thus, in the 1970 Preface to *A Tree for Poverty*, she explains that she had begun the translations in 1952 and deprecates them as amateurish because she herself had been much younger and naïve. A look to the bibliographical details on the immediately opposite page informs us that the book of translations from Somali oral culture was first published in Nairobi in 1954.

Whatever her sense of her own limitations, Laurence's small volume of translations is significant historically and in literary terms. Laurence has written that "For me, the doing of it was a labour of love" (*Camel Bell* 225). But *A Tree for Poverty* is much, much more. It is the first translation into English and collection of Somali poems and folk-tales. In terms, therefore, of the study of African literature, the volume is analogous to those late eighteenth- and early nineteenth-century archaeologies of folk-culture, the oral tradition, of central and western Europe. Modern British literature begins with the Romantic delving into the songs, ballads, and the anonymous but communally-shared folk-tales of the countryside. So, too, does the contemporary history of much Commonwealth writing, and *A Tree for Poverty* is a model of its kind.

The introductory essays on the range, themes, styles, modes and oratorical conventions of Somali literature are a fine place to start, if one wishes to study the gradual awareness in Commonwealth literary criticism that, without adequate understanding of oral discourse, indigenous non-metropolitan cultures will be silenced and marginalized yet again. In Canadian studies, for example, we are still desperately in need of scholars and writers who, as a "labour of love," will show us how the tales and communal traditions of our own native peoples can and do invest a culture with dignity and grace. Anthropologists tell us that we need field-workers with a sense of literature, and literary scholars working in this area will explain that we need an entire repertoire of rhetorical skills to convey the performance of these texts.

Laurence's essay at the start of *A Tree for Poverty* is a foundational text in that enterprise. But one needn't feel displaced by such rigorously moral and intellectual demands. In *The Prophet's Camel Bell*, Laurence offers yet another way past the unfortunately locked door of pre-textual cultures. She explains how she first had to win the confidence and trust of Hersi, a Somali worker who became his community's storyteller each night around the campfires when she and her husband, and other whites, were supposedly looking somewhere else. Once she had cajoled him into commenting on someone else's story, Hersi performed almost exclusively for her. As she describes his manner, Laurence suggests yet another way to annotate such shamanistic performances. She also announces, it would seem, the role model for her own work:

> Every afternoon, when he was not needed at the work site, Hersi came to the brushwood hut. He told the stories to me in English, with an admixture of Somali and Arabic, for such English words as "saint" and

> "angel" were unknown to him, but I knew the Somali or Arabic equivalent. Although most of the labourers and drivers did not speak much English, there was always an audience. They drifted into the hut quietly, those who were off duty, and listened. They did not understand many of the words, but they recognized the familiar tales by the way in which Hersi acted them out.
>
> For me, also, his acting had tremendous value. It compensated to some extent for the fact that I was not hearing the stories in Somali, in which he would have been able to express them with better style. Hersi belonged to that ancient brotherhood of born storytellers. He played by turns the different roles in the tale, transforming himself by some alchemy of expression or stance into whatever he chose—a saint or a sultan, a thief craftily plotting how to outwit a naïve tribesman. He told me the story of the three wise counsellors—three hashish addicts whom a disgruntled sultan called in when his regular counsellors had all failed him. And for this moment, Hersi became the hashish addicts, dreamily twirling in their narcotic dance. When he told me of Arawailo, he made me see the barbaric splendour and the cruelty of that fabled queen. He told me of Deg-Der, the cannibal woman, and I could visualize her horrible countenance and her donkey's ear. He was not himself at these times. He was so carried away by his stories that he lived them, taking on the characters like cloaks. . . . When he finished, he would be exhausted and would have to be revived with a mug of strong spiced tea, for he was an artist and he gave to each performance the very best of which he was capable. (*Camel Bell* 159-60)

In *A Tree for Poverty* and its later companion piece, *The Prophet's Camel Bell*, Laurence thus explains just how the tales and poems are performed in an oral culture, what their social and ethical import in that culture are, and then offers us an introduction to some of those performance pieces.

One can therefore say that her first literary work—translating Somali poems and folk-tales—determines utterly the scope and range of her last and greatest achievement, *The Diviners*. She is, at the beginning and end of her writing career, concerned with orality and the transmissions of culture beyond and outside books. She is always concerned with what are holy words, technologies of the sacred, shaman songs, words of various diviners in different parts of the world. In *The Prophet's Camel Bell*, she explains her insight and inadvertently defines her life's mission:

> Every culture in the world passes on knowledge to the next generation, but the nature of that knowledge suits the survival requirements of each particular place. . . . We put our confidence in technical knowledge. They appeared to put their confidence in ritual. (138-39)

These folk-tales and ancient songs, which are so comical and rich, so integral to Laurence's understanding of the Otherness of Somali, and all non-imperialist culture by extension, are the early models for her later renditions of Métis oral traditions through Jules Tonnerre's legends and Pique's songs which she takes from both her parents' traditions on her personal quest for identity in the Canadian west.

Similarly, a reading of *Long Drums and Cannons* cannot but astonish the reader granted the hindsight of the present. The book is historically significant, and sheds further light on Laurence's literary mission in Manawaka and environs. The introduction of the preface is again specific and informed. If *A Tree for Poverty* was a labour of love in the 1950s, *Long Drums and Cannons* is that, too, as well as the product of an informed reader's eye and ear. What is striking is just how exact and scrupulous, and therefore undated, Laurence's judgements, insights and explanations are. She gets it right every time, and with each writer she discusses.

As a teacher and critic of African literature since the late

1970s, what I find most surprising about this 1968 publication is the astuteness with which she sets about organizing her examination of Nigerian literature. Quite rightly, she begins by suggesting Amos Tutuola's *The Palm-Wine Drinkard* (1952) as the founding text of this new literary tradition. Tutuola's "novel" is many things: I've taught it in a course on myth and tragedy in contemporary literature, and my students at UBC have delighted in its fusion of pidgin and English, oral narrative conventions and sophisticated high-modernism. For Laurence, it's an important text because it operates at the intersection of indigenous Yoruba folk-tale and imported European conventions of the novel and indeed literate culture.

As she points out in her introduction, Tutuola's works have had a farther-ranging audience than many writers even dream of achieving ever since T.S. Eliot at Faber and Faber first bought the manuscript and published it as a breakthrough to some new kind of style, new kind of dialect and new kind of literary artefact. Laurence is far more matter-of-fact: "Contemporary Nigerian literature really dates from that time . . . a new literature which has drawn sustenance both from traditional oral literature and from the present and rapidly changing society" (*Long Drums* 8). At this point in her essay, she digresses into a discussion of the importance of small presses, the central position of literary journals in Nigeria, and the nurturing of a national literary tradition at university campuses across the country. It is very clear, too, that Laurence has read widely in these journals, and investigated personally the scholarship she commends.

What is important for our consideration, however, is just how closely her descriptions of the emergence and strengths of Nigerian literature in its earliest days resemble our contemporary understanding of our own literary traditions and culture. We, too, stress the importance of small, regional presses: indeed, they are often the only presses these days not controlled by foreign money and therefore willing to take chances by publishing manuscripts presented by eager unknowns. And, as we all remember, Morag Gunn's early dilemma in *The Diviners* is how to become a writer when the imperial tradition not only occupies the classroom and the textbooks, but also demands the right to edit and revise the manuscripts of would-be national writers. As Laurence suggests, even a luminary like Nigeria's Nobel laureate, Wole Soyinka, began as just such an eager unknown. Significantly, her chapter on his drama, "Voices of Life, Dance of Death," opens *Long Drums and Cannons*: it is still a very solid and impressively informed introduction to this solid and impressive writer.

Again, literary journals here—such as *Canadian Literature* from UBC—are crucial to the maintenance and nurturing of our literary culture and intellectual life. Finally, however much we may pride ourselves on being advanced and progressive, the study of our national literary traditions is even more recent a phenomenon in Canada than is the study of Nigerian literature at Nigerian universities. And, unlike the situation which prevails in anglophone African universities, a student in a Department of English can graduate from a Canadian university without having encountered any national literature. Thus, at an important time in our own national history, Laurence describes the situation of an African literature emerging from the shadows of imperialism: what we read, in hindsight, is a description of our common heritage as Commonwealth nations.

The list of writers she selects to represent the range of styles and themes and the manner of Nigerian literature is again very accurate. With a clear eye and ear, she chooses the greats at a time when some of them have yet to prove their full competence and achievement. It's an ambitious list, and a level-headed assessment. Achebe's work, for example, is singled out for its clear articulation of the writer's responsibility in every society, but most especially in those cultures which have not been able to identify their domestic traditions very clearly. In Achebe, this dilemma is clearly attributed as a legacy of colonialism.

Laurence's discussion of Achebe's historical novels is thoughtfully considered and far-reaching. *Things Fall Apart* is rightly seen as ironic, and complex because of that irony: a novel which articulates the clash between European and African cultures, this 1958 cornerstone and masterpiece of early Commonwealth literature is now translated into over thirty languages, and taught internationally in literature, history and anthropology courses. Laurence cannot recommend Achebe's work highly enough: *Arrow of God* (1964) is "one of the best novels written anywhere in the past decade" (*Long Drums* 111). She praises it for its analyses of the difficulties of human communication across cultures, and across generations, and for its transformation of metropolitan English into a local, regional, and therefore universal dialect of contemporary literature.

I will return to these claims presently, when I discuss Laurence's short stories from Africa. But I must first stress that the critical terms with which Laurence describes Achebe's early achievement prefigure her own Manawaka cycle of novels. That is, Canadian literature is the sleeping giant behind the description of Nigerian literature in *Long Drums and Cannons*. And clearly, but again in retrospect, Laurence's critical endeavours on behalf of African literature determine what it is she will attempt on returning to Canada. I know of no other work on Commonwealth literature which so consistently links cultures and literatures which contemporary study and popular preconception would otherwise sunder.

In retrospect, I am most surprised to find Laurence recommending the works of Elechi Amadi and Gabriel Okara for our consideration. Both writers had to wait almost ten years before the significance of their prose fictions was academically enshrined in the study of Nigerian and Commonwealth literature. Laurence, however, is sharp and unhesitating. And, again, one cannot help but read the future integrity of the Manawaka novels in her comments about these superficially so different texts.

Amadi's *The Concubine* (1966) is now recognized as the clearest distillation of traditional village life before European contact in Nigerian and perhaps African literature. Laurence describes its style and tragic mode, and then explores the ideological implications of Amadi's nostalgic heroics. She praises its "unfaltering authenticity" and discerns how such rootedness in the particular and the local helps to "extend the novel's meaning beyond any one culture" (*Long Drums* 177). What most impresses, however, are its pastoral qualities—"some of the best descriptions of a village in all of Nigerian writing" (*Long Drums* 182-83)—and the ultimate conclusion that, even in the depths of human despair, "victory . . . does not entirely belong to the gods" (*Long Drums* 184).

Okara's *The Voice* (1964) is a similarly eccentric inclusion in Laurence's estimation of Nigerian literature. Recognized now and admired for its linguistic dexterities, *The Voice* met initial silence upon its publication. Okara's achievement demands some critical explication, some mediation, before the reader can understand what is happening in the text. What is happening is that Okara, a poet in the mould of Hopkins and classical musician by vocation, has appropriated the full armament of stylistic, imagistic and rhetorical and syntactic strategies available to the writer in English and fashioned a novel which allows the reader the sense and feel of speaking and using an entirely different language: Okara's mother-tongue, Ijaw. To search for an analogy here, one must go—I believe—to Synge's passionate, tragic dialect of Gaelic in English which heralded the decolonization of literature at the turn of the century. Laurence praises Okara's novel for its poetic qualities, describes the linguistic system of the Ijaw people, and recognizes the ideological sympathies with Okara's protagonist which her own women will later articulate. She describes the novel as

> an individual's questioning of the established values, his need to relate the inner truth to the outer reality . . . in search of what he calls it—the truth, honesty, some genuine contact with others. He dares to question the existing order of things and to suggest that there is more in life than the circumscribed laws of the tribe. To the village chief and elders, Okolo represents a great threat, and they attempt to discredit him by calling him mad. (*Long Drums* 193-94)

If one were writing a blurb to print on the latest printing of *The Diviners* or perhaps *A Jest of God*, one could do worse than use these words of Laurence to describe another's quest.

But what interests me most about Margaret Laurence's critical sojourn among Nigerian novels and plays is the effect such reading and thinking about a new national literature had upon her sense of her place in Canada, and of her own writing. In *Heart of a Stranger*, for example, she explains what she had already written in Somaliland, and how living as an outsider in foreign, often exotic, places and coming to learn about another culture is always the study of our own culture and our own traditions. She opens that autobiographical collection with reminiscence and the empowering sense of identity which came to her through expatriation:

> I have spent a good many years of my adult life as a stranger in strange lands, in some cases as a resident, and in others as a traveller. I have met suspicion and mistrust at times, and I have also met with warmth and generosity. The process of trying to understand people of another culture—their concepts, their customs, their life-view—is a fascinating and complex one, sometimes frustrating, never easy, but in the long run enormously rewarding. One thing I learned, however, was that my experience of other countries probably taught me more about myself and even my own land than it did about anything else. . . . I began to write out of my own background only after I had lived some years away, and

> when I finally came back to Canada to stay, nearly ten years after I had returned in my fiction, I knew for certain that it was where I belonged, and I knew why. (*Heart* 11)

Finally I want to briefly sketch what I think is the itinerary which moved Laurence from critical studies and translations of African literatures, through early fictional ventures, to concentrate her energies on becoming the bard and chronicler of Prairie life and Western identity and, in the process, to found a tradition of Canadian literature which must be read as part of the family tree of Commonwealth literatures she so carefully tended while abroad. To do so, I will concentrate my efforts on her 1963 collection of stories, *The Tomorrow-Tamer*—a book clearly positioned between Manawaka, London, Somaliland and West Africa. In order to develop a sense of my theoretical model, I will refer to four stories from that collection: "The Tomorrow-Tamer," "The Merchant of Heaven," "The Drummer of All the World," and "The Perfume Sea." Perhaps, too, the order in which I have selected them reveals what I am about to suggest.

If I were to name the genre or convention which best describes the power and effect of "The Tomorrow-Tamer," it would have to be ventriloquism. This magnificent tale bears no indication that I can find after several readings that its author is not one of the new generation of African writers whom she praises and brings to our attention through her studies of their fictions in *Long Drums and Cannons*. It is an exquisitely caught literary moment, where the sophisticated armoury of style and rhetoric are deployed in the service of pre-literate, oral culture and against the dereliction which the advancing technologies of progress and independence have foisted upon village life internationally.

Indeed, "The Tomorrow-Tamer" reads very like a story by Achebe, or by one of the young Ghanaian writers whose works no doubt Laurence also knew. Whereas some of the stories in the collection have been described as apprentice-work by other critics of Canadian literature, this—with its high-arching and tremendously moving conclusion—is fully achieved and densely moving. It is, however, most eccentric and perhaps somewhat baroque. A Canadian writer of Anglo-Scots background has so completely lost herself in a richly sensual, but utterly alien, culture that her narrative bears little if any trace of her own provenance. "The Tomorrow-Tamer" magically conveys the sense of ritual and well-being, of rightness, in a way of life and being forever closed to every outsider, and to anyone—for that matter—who can play with words and writing. This is simply the very best African story written by a non-African writer I've ever encountered.

"The Merchant of Heaven" and "The Drummer of All the World" are more obviously akin to Laurence's Anglo-Scots Canadian identity. The first is, above all else, strenuously moral in its own roundabout fashion. Brother Lemon cannot accept an indigenous image of a world-saviour, and Christianity—as represented by missionaries in the tropics—is thus found severely wanting in human sympathy and understanding. Again, this is a compassionate reading: Laurence works by implication and guides the reader to confront racism, rather than announcing the blindnesses of all imperialisms.

"The Drummer of All the World" is a more ambitious, less predictable enterprise. Its experimental style—the text broken into blocks which the reader follows, and the critic examines for coherence and method—and its underlying symbolism mark it off in the collection. Laurence attempts to write across racial divides: another concern which resurfaces in her last and greatest novel. Some have commented that they find the story awkward and inconclusive. To me this story is the kind of fiction which allows those of us who live in Canada the opportunity to begin to imagine what being white and connected to Africa might mean—in terms of strife, anger and resentment as well as pain, commitment and thwarted love. But she also explicitly announces her awareness of the presumption of talking or writing in the place of African peoples. Here, therefore, Laurence connects with South African literature by white writers such as Doris Lessing and Nadine Gordimer.

"The Perfume Sea" is my favourite story in the collection, both intellectually and stylistically. I find it a gentle, compelling, ironic, and wry study of expatriate life. Unlike most white Africans, Mr. Archipelago and Doree do stay on after independence and the loss of power and prestige. There is humour in that neither had much of either before independence. After independence they cannot quite pay the rent, or even reveal their pasts; but these two odd characters—perhaps prefiguring the grotesques which Laurence uses in her later fictions to comment on the dominant culture and to nurture a writer: Christy and Prin—are neither angry, morose nor pathetic. They belong, quite simply, nowhere and everywhere. And due to happy accidents of fate, they will survive. Even in such a seemingly slight, but movingly affective, piece, Laurence is compassionate and instructive. Doree and Archipelago, like the characters to come on the Prairies and in the city, are not passive: they await their opportunities aggressively, and leap at the chance of new lives.

The question I have set myself is: how is the Africa of Laurence's criticism, translations, travel memoirs, and earliest fictions connected to and the precursor of her Canadian fictions? The answer is everywhere apparent. The African cultures which she inhabited as visitor and guest affected her emotionally and intellectually. The most obvious proof is the critical labours she engaged in to bring those cultures to a wider audience. Africa moved her to read and study human cultures, and revealed the connectedness of people to place.

Where others might celebrate difference and cultural aphasia, Laurence writes clearly and unembarrassedly about the necessary interconnectedness of people, and the place of myth and ritual in all our lives. Her African experience could very easily have been the catalyst for social comedy. Laurence herself explains the recognition of the impulse, and the various acts of compassion which moved her own writing beyond such provincialisms. Africa, to Margaret Laurence, quite simply meant coming home to Canada:

> I found the sahib-type English so detestable that I always imagined that if I ever wrote a book about Somaliland, it would give me tremendous joy to deliver a withering blast of invective in their direction. Strangely, I now find I cannot do so. What holds me back is not pity for them, although they were certainly pitiable, but rather the feeling that in thoroughly exposing such of their sores as I saw, there would be something obscene and pointless, like mutilating a corpse. For these people are dead, actually, although some of them will continue to lumber around Africa for a few more years, like lost dinosaurs. They bear no relation to most parts of Africa today, and however much Africans may have suffered at their hands, it is to be hoped that one day Africans may be able to see them for what they really were—not people who were motivated by a brutally strong belief in their own superiority, but people who were so desperately uncertain of their own worth and their ability to cope within their own societies that they were forced to seek some kind of mastery in a place where all the cards were stacked in their favour and where they could live in a self-generated glory by transferring all evils, all weaknesses, on to another people. As long as they could be scornful or fearful of Africa or Africans, they could avoid the possibility of being scornful or fearful of anything within themselves. (*Camel Bell* 205)

Works Consulted

Laurence, Margaret. *Heart of a Stranger*. Toronto: McClelland and Stewart, 1976.

__________. *Long Drums and Cannons: Nigerian dramatists and novelists, 1952-1966*. London and Toronto: Macmillan, 1968.

__________. *The Prophet's Camel Bell*. Toronto: McClelland and Stewart, 1963.

__________. *This Side Jordan*. London: Macmillan and Co. Ltd., and New York: St. Martin's Press, 1960.

__________. *The Tomorrow-Tamer*. London: Macmillan and Co. Ltd., 1963.

__________. *A Tree for Poverty: Somali Poetry and Prose*. Nairobi: 1954. Hamilton: McMaster University Press, and Dublin: Irish University Press, 1970.

David Williams
University of Manitoba

Jacob and the Demon: Hagar as Storyteller in *The Stone Angel*

All perform their tragic play. . . .
Yet they, should the last scene be there,
The great stage curtain about to drop,
If worthy their prominent part in the play,
Do not break up their lines to weep.
They know that Hamlet and Lear are gay;
Gaiety transfiguring all that dread.
—W.B. Yeats, "Lapis Lazuli"

i

I HAVE HEARD certain post-modernists say they are sick of art that confesses fault, that writes our weakness in the same old way.

It's not the heroine of *The Stone Angel* who's old and decrepit, they say. It's the form. For gawd's sake, why not just teach *True Confessions*?

Don't do that. You could get pregnant.

But they lied to you, can't you see? The authorities always lie. How else do parents control their children? Thou shalt not. Because.

" 'There's not a decent girl in this town would wed without her family's consent,' he said. 'It's not done.' 'It'll be done by me,' I said, drunk with exhilaration at my daring" (*SA* 49).

Yet rebels come to bad ends. Unless they confess that father knows best. Even belatedly.

Well, they lied to you. Don't you know that parents envy their children? You have to forget those old wives' tales. Remember that fiction is always fiction. *The Diviners*, now there's a model for writers. It's a story about story, process instead of product. The teller lets you know it's not the truth. "It's all true and not true. Isn't that a bugger, now?" (*Div* 88).

So how does imagination give the lie to historical determinism? "A popular misconception is that we can't change the past—everyone is constantly changing their own past, recalling it, revising it. What really happened? A meaningless question" (*Div* 60). No one has to be hostage to history any more. If you don't like it, remember it differently. Memory is a two-way street. Uh, river. Whatever. They're all "totally invented memories" (*Div* 10).

So the past is open to change. But what about the present? "Morag grows and learns, particularly in her relationship with Christie, throughout the second narrative level [the past], but does not move toward a significant character development on the first level; she has, in a way . . . already 'arrived' when the novel begins. . . . Nor can the reader see her change because of what she learns from her memories. This latter condition is true because Morag not only understands herself, she understands the memory process" (Gom 56).

For an open-ended novel, *The Diviners* is strangely enamoured of circles. For one thing, the end is already realized in the beginning. We are told that "Something about Pique's going . . . was unresolved in Morag's mind" (*Div* 5). But memory returns to the loss of her own parents to show what is really unresolved in Morag's mind. Colin Gunn's going, and his wife Louisa's, is the root of Morag's problem. Morag being left. The lost child is the mother, not the daughter. And so the "child" has all the answers before the end of the first chapter. "Perhaps I only want their forgiveness for having forgotten them. I remember their deaths, but not their lives. Yet they're inside me, flowing unknown in my blood and moving unrecognized in my skull" (*Div* 19). It doesn't take much to realize that Pique will continue Morag's life on similar terms. "As for Morag, it is interesting that the reader takes leave of her . . . where he had first met her: watching the river that flows both ways and looking 'ahead into the past, and back into the future, until the silence' " (Gom 57).

So the form of *The Diviners* comes round again to determinism. Blood will out, with books as with people. The family likeness to *The Stone Angel* was inescapable. " 'You take after me,' he said, as though that made everything clear. 'You've got backbone, I'll give you that' " (*SA* 10). "I tried to shut my ears to it, and thought I had, yet years later, when I was rearing my two boys, I found myself saying the same words to them" (*SA* 13). For no one really escapes the past, as Hagar is forced to admit. She runs away to a weathered grey fish cannery only to find herself in Bram's house, John and Arlene's vacated home. Now Morag, she had the sense to quit running a long time ago. She's already come full circle. There she sits like Janus, looking both ways.

The Janus-faced writer helps to improve on the technique of the earlier novel. "It is the form of *The Stone Angel*, with its two parallel plot lines and two Hagars, that *The Diviners* uses most as its model . . . [Here] Laurence has preserved the technique of *The Stone Angel* and legitimized it" (Gom 50, 52). Of course, Morag has an excuse that the old woman can't have in stringing memories together like beads on a string. Morag writes her memories in a notebook. Even the most ardent supporters of *The Stone Angel* are prone to confess that memory doesn't work like a novel unfolding. Hagar's greatest sin is that she isn't a novelist.

Writing a novel is Morag's declaration of independence. She breaks away from the husband who refuses children by writing herself into her blind protagonist: "Lilac has aborted herself in a way that Morag recalls from long ago. And yet it is not Eva for whom Morag experiences pain now—it is Lilac only, at this moment" (*Div* 229). Morag's husband "cannot ever say to her, finally, once and for all, that he cannot bear for her to bear a child" (*Div* 246). The most he dares to ask is whether "the main character—Lilac—expresses anything which we haven't known before?" (*Div* 246). The question is most unfair to the younger writer: Morag learns that Lilac's aborted child is her own. But the older writer has little to express beside her "River of Now" which we haven't known before from her "River of Then."

"That incredibly moving statement—'What strength I have's mine own, Which is most faint—' If only he can hang onto that knowledge, that would be true strength" (*Div* 330), Morag writes to her friend Ella. Yet, because Morag discovers herself through the stories she has made, her knowing cannot be lost as easily as her future *making*. The figure of Prospero announces this terrible concern with lost doing. So Morag rehearses, for herself as much as us, the old story of her making. For us, it is all new; we are taken through the stages of her growing strength. But for Morag, it is old hat; she knows the whole story before it ever begins. No wonder she can't grow any more in the telling.

Now Hagar, at the end of her life, would like to tell away the threat of endings. Yet Hagar grows in her telling. But how? When even she announces herself at the mercy of God or fate or some other teller, not at all free to make what she will of herself? "Now I light one of my cigarettes and stump around my room, remembering furiously, for no reason except that I am caught up in it" (*SA* 6). Hagar is caught up by her author, it would seem, who spirits her through time like the Ghost of Christmas Past. Rubbing her nose in it. Until she cries uncle: "Pride was my wilderness, and the demon that led me there was fear" (*SA* 292).

Pride goeth before a fall. All the critics defer to the proverb. " 'Pride was my wilderness'—strength was my weakness—is Hagar's moment of truth" (Thomas 68-69). "Hagar's life represents a progress from one displaced garden to another until the realization comes to her that her pride has kept her from joy and live [sic], has created the wilderness which has been her life" (Thompson 96). "Although Hagar's pride is a wilderness because it isolates her from human contact, it also proves a basis for moral awareness" (Kertzer 504). Hagar, however, confesses that it was really a demon who left her in a wilderness of pride, that Fear is his name, and that his numbers are legion. But demons are a hell of a thing to face in criticism. Proverbs offer refuge.

Pride, not a proverb, is Hagar's refuge. Pride keeps the demon at bay. "Above the town, on the hill brow, the stone angel used to stand. I wonder if she stands there yet, in memory of her who relinquished her feeble ghost as I gained my stubborn one, my mother's angel that my father bought in pride to mark her bones and proclaim his dynasty, as he fancied it, forever and a day" (*SA* 3). Pride saves Hagar, as it saves her father, from the taint of the dead mother. Weakness, she sees, is fatal. No wonder she cannot put on her mother's shawl to comfort her dying brother: " 'Hagar—put it on and hold him for awhile.' I stiffened and drew away my hands. 'I can't. Oh Matt, I'm sorry, but I can't, I can't. I'm not a bit like her' " (*SA* 25). Identification is just as fatal.

In memory of her. Though Hagar will not stoop to her father's hypocrisy, her "memorial" cannot recall a mother that she never knew. So she holds to this marble surrogate who is blankly reassuring. The stone angel abides where her mother does not. It is her own proud front against the fear of death, against the fear that she has taken that life: "It seemed to me then that Matt was almost apologetic, as though he felt he ought to tell me he didn't blame me for her dying, when in his heart he really did" (*SA* 24-25). She can't let her guard down now; the feeble mother has to be changed into something strong. Into a woman more like Hagar's father.

"Father didn't hold it against me that it had happened so. I know, because he told me. Perhaps he thought it was a fair exchange, her life for mine" (*SA* 59). The child naturally blames the victim, being powerless herself. Her only hope is to exchange her identity. Since her father has fashioned an enduring image of his lost wife, she makes herself over in the same pattern. The helpless daughter becomes the invincible wife.

The "wife" isn't merely playing at being Electra. The attraction to Daddy is the nature of his strength. "Auntie Doll was always telling us that Father was a God-fearing man. I never for a moment believed it, of course. I couldn't imagine Father fearing anyone, God included, especially when he didn't even owe his existence to the Almighty. God might have created heaven and earth and the majority of people, but Father was a self-made man, as he himself had told us often enough" (*SA* 17). To be self-made is to be subject to no power outside the self, not even Death. 'Tis a consummation devoutly to be wished.

So "Hagar flees death in various ways. By retreating to the past she is, of course, attempting to escape her future, her impending death. In memory, at least, she can be a young girl, a new bride, a mother" (Davidson 65). But memory is more than a safe retreat. It is a means of inventing a new history. Otherwise the dead mother taints everything with her mortality. "But all I could think of was that meek woman I'd never seen, the woman Dan was said to resemble so much and from whom he'd inherited a frailty I could not help but detest, however much a part of me wanted to sympathize. To play at being her—it was beyond me" (*SA* 25). Instead, she plays at being the self-made man: her father, who dies like everybody else.

In retrospect, Jason Currie's death should justify Hagar's war of independence. "Within a year, Currie Memorial Park was started beside the Wachakwa river. The scrub oak was uprooted and the crabgrass mown, and nearly circular beds of petunias proclaimed my father's immortality in mauve and pink frilled petals. Even now, I detest petunias" (*SA* 63-64). For the self-made man hasn't made himself to last. Petunias are a poor substitute for immortality.

Hagar's problem at the end of her life is the same as it was at the beginning—how to create an enduring image of herself. The paternal image is powerless to save her; and the maternal one is deadly. What she needs is nothing less than a metamorphosis. "The night my son died I was transformed to stone and never wept at all" (*SA* 243). As in life, so in story. She represses the painful truth of human mortality and starts her story over with the image of a woman "transformed to stone." The weeping mother, Niobe, who was changed to stone by her grief is here transformed because she will not weep. Stone outlives the cause of tears. By telling her story to herself, Hagar creates the indestructible self that she yearns to be. But "Hagar's vaunted strength is a sham" (Davidson 65). The sham is what makes her story so compelling. For she is driven to deconstruct it. And then to recreate it in terms of her newly confessed weakness.

ii

"I'd be about six, surely," the memoir finds its ground in what looks like simple chronology. "There was I . . . haughty, hoity-toity, Jason Currie's black-haired daughter. . . . [My father] never believed in wasting a word or a minute. He was a self-made man" (*SA* 6-7). "I'd be about eight," the self-made woman wastes few words herself in confirming the point of the lesson: "Auntie Doll was always telling us that Father was a God-fearing man . . ." (*SA* 16). What the neat chronology enacts is this imitation of her father. Memory shapes a model to free her of her mother's ghost.

The self-made man still contradicts, at points, his own theology: "I'd been named, hopefully, for a well-to-do spinster great-aunt in Scotland, who, to my father's chagrin, had left her money to the Humane Society" (*SA* 14). Heritage is not to be denied where there's a dollar to be made. But family history repeats the lesson Father learned the hard way: "You were named after him, Dan. Sir Daniel Currie—the title died with him, for it wasn't a baronetcy. . . . His partner cheated him—oh, it was a bad affair all around, I can tell you, and there was I, without a hope or a ha'penny" (*SA* 14-15). *There was I.* The passive construction is the same one Hagar uses. One is left at the mercy of one's inheritance. Better to take it all back, to start from scratch. "He called me 'miss' when he was displeased, and 'daughter' when he felt kindly disposed toward me. Never Hagar" (*SA* 14). The name itself is too painful to be borne. The outcast Hagar must be unnamed.

The daughter, however, has learned her father's lesson too well. She must reject him to be truly like him. Her husband offers her a means to be free of her relational identity: "I was Hagar to him, and if he were alive, I'd be Hagar to him yet. And now I think he was the only person close to me who ever thought of me by my name, not daughter, nor sister, nor mother, nor even wife, but Hagar, always" (*SA* 80). And Hagar she remains, unique and unattached, almost to the end of her days: "Stupid old baggage, who do you think you are? *Hagar*. There's no one like me in this world" (*SA* 250).

The trouble is, she marries a man named Bram. There's no one like him, either. But Abram and Hagar together are an old story. And the story ends badly, with Hagar outcast again. What's a girl to do? It's almost as if there *is* a God, at any rate an author, imposing a pattern from above. Hagar, suspecting the former, quarrels with the Father, resisting her creator. She has to unmake the old story.

"As we can see from the uncompromising portrait of Hagar's husband Bram ('Abram'), [Laurence's] use of the Genesis story is not simply as an allegory of the Genesis text" (Jeffrey 92). Hagar, in fact, is quite prepared to forget all about Genesis. Abram's first wife is dead. There is no Sara for her to mock and jeer at in her barrenness, but there is also no Sara to drive her out into the wilderness. The child could be a problem, though, wanting to be born. "What could I say? That I'd not wanted children? That I believed I was going to die, and wished I would, and prayed I wouldn't? That the child he wanted would be his, and none of mine?" (*SA* 100). Mothers are supposed to die. Or at least be exiled. And if they live? There's still that old threat of endings. Rewrite the story, then. Have Hagar, not Abram, drive the child into exile. Marvin, be Ishmael.

The second son is obviously Isaac, God's promised child to Sara. Henceforth, Hagar, be Sara. Not as the type of God's promised Covenant, Abram's wife, but as the antitype, the Virgin Mother: "I wasn't frightened at all when John was born. I knew I wouldn't die that time. Bram had gone to fix a fence down by the slough. Such mercies aren't often afforded us. I hitched up and drove the buggy into town myself. . . . Calm as a stout madonna" (*SA* 122). There's the ultimate proof you're self-made. Even your husband can't make you. The invincible wife becomes the inviolable mother. The bondswoman Hagar accomplishes her own allegory. She will live happily ever after, without her husband. Death, be not proud.

Death still has dominion, though. The husband goes swiftly downhill and nearly takes his wife with him: "I stood for a long time, looking, wondering how a person could change so much and never see it. . . . The face—a brown and leathery face that wasn't mine. Only the eyes were mine, staring as though to pierce the lying glass and get beneath to some truer image, infinitely distant" (*SA* 133). She has to leave her old man in order to recover her true self: "When I reached Bram, I saw how old he'd grown. His mouth opened when he saw me, and all I remember noticing was that his teeth had developed brown ridges at the front. We walked out of the store together, down the steps, past wrinkled Charlie Bean, gaping and shivering in his vigil, and that was the last time we ever walked anywhere together, Brampton Shipley and myself" (*SA* 135). Hagar's not going to be anybody's old lady. She exiles Abram to the wilderness.

The wife is drawn back all the same to her husband's deathbed. She can't explain it. She goes. When she finds out that Bram had loved her after all, she rages as usual against fate: "I could not speak for the salt that filled my throat, and for anger—not at anyone, at God, perhaps, for giving us eyes but almost never sight" (*SA* 173). She sees nonetheless with blinding sight that sexual love is a coupling with death: "He lay curled up and fragile in the big bed where we'd coupled and it made me sick to think I'd lain with him, for now he looked like an ancient child" (*SA* 183). She can only deny the act, as she did before: "Didn't I betray myself in rising sap, like a heedless and compelled maple after a winter? But no. He never expected any such a thing, and so he never perceived it. I prided myself upon keeping my pride intact, like some maidenhead" (*SA* 81). Pride saves her from a sexual fall. The Virgin can have no carnal knowledge of Death.

When Hagar leaves Bram behind in the final wilderness, she seems to run right out of the Old Testament story. But the threat of determinism has crept up on her again by the time she runs away from Marvin's house. At the fish cannery she finds "an old brass scale, the kind they used to use for weighing letters or pepper. It tips and tilts to my finger, but the brass weights are lost. Nothing can be weighed here and found wanting" (*SA* 154). MENE, MENE, TEKEL, UPHARSIN. Thou art weighed in the balances, and art found wanting. Nothing to do with me, she shrugs like her father. That's the Book of Daniel. The judgement of Belshazzar is another story.

The irony of Hagar's memoir, of course, is that she's so determined to forget. Though who could forget a dead son? She has to substitute Marvin for the son who dies: "I had two [sons]. One was killed—in the last war" (*SA* 104). So too she substitutes a secular story for the Biblical one which has threatened her freedom: "I recalled part of a poem today—can I recall the rest? I search, but it evades me, and then all at once the last part returns and I repeat the lines. They give me courage, more than if I'd recited the Twenty-third Psalm, but why this should be so, I cannot tell" (*SA* 162-63). Telling might expose the whole charade. For the Good Book does not lead a woman named Hagar to lie down beside still waters; it leaves her in a desert. If she happens to find herself in the wilderness anyway, she'd be happier with a folk-tale. Henceforth be Meg Merrilies.

Keats's homeless gipsy offers a saving image to the friendless woman. "In choosing to recall the disreputable gipsy instead of the psalmist, Hagar seems to be following a romantic side of her nature, often repressed but as intrinsic to it as her stony pride" (Coldwell 94). Hagar's "romantic side" continues, however, to exalt respectability over instinct. In modelling herself after Meg Merrilies, she is both preserving appearance and repressing truth. The source of her comfort is most evident in lines she neglects to quote:

Her brothers were the craggy hills
Her sisters larchen trees;
Alone with her great family
She lived as she did please.

The woman who has rejected family creates a fiction of her retreat to it. But Hagar is not the sister of all nature, nor is the stone angel (as is the Amazon) a benefactor of poor cottagers. The image of the gipsy is simply her excuse to "live as she did please."

Only when Hagar is forced to remember John's death does the Biblical story overcome her repression: "I was not thinking at all, not at all, and yet I recall some words that must have spun, unspoken, through me at that moment. *If he should die, let me not see it*" (*SA* 241).

> And she went, and sat her down over against him a good way off, as it were a bowshot: for she said, Let me not see the death of the child. And she sat over against him, and lifted up her voice, and wept.
>
> And God heard the voice of the lad; and the angel of God called to Hagar out of heaven, and said unto her, What aileth thee, Hagar? fear not; for God hath heard the voice of the lad where he is.
>
> Arise, lift up the lad, and hold him in thine hand; for I will make him a great nation.
>
> And God opened her eyes, and she saw a well of water; and she went, and filled the bottle with water, and gave the lad drink. (*AV*, Gen. xxi: 16-19)

"It's all true and not true. Isn't that a bugger, now?"

There is no longer any voice from heaven to save the lad. Just Murray Ferney Lees standing in for the philanthropic Meg Merrilies. And there's no one to save his lad, either.

But Hagar's eyes are opened all the same. Murray shows her a well of forgiveness in her wilderness of pride. Memory serves at last to confront her demon Fear. But the truth is that she has hastened her fatal identity with the Biblical Hagar. Only when she sees it does she find that she's misread the whole story of Abraham. For there is another side to the family history that she hasn't even begun to learn to tell.

iii

Ich weiss nicht was soll es bedeuten . . .
Dass ich so traurig bin . . .
Ein Märchen aus uralten Zeiten . . .
Das geht mir nicht aus dem Sinn— (*SA* 256-57)

The song of Heine's boatman sounds alien, yet somehow familiar, in the chorus of voices which plead away the night in Hagar's hospital ward. Alien to Hagar, because there is no evidence in the novel that she understands a word of German. More familiar, perhaps, to a reader who wants to find in this song and Reverend Troy's hymn "a binary structure to make clearer the hermeneutic of the whole" (Jeffrey 96):

I don't know what it means
That I have been so saddened;
A tale out of olden times
That I cannot fully understand. (Jeffrey 96)

Still, the boatman perplexed by the song of the sirens is not a very good gloss on Hagar's predicament. Heine's only hidden relevance for us is the part about being bewildered by an old tale. "I wish he could have looked like Jacob then, wrestling with the angel and besting it, wringing a blessing from it with his might. But no. He sweated and grunted angrily" (*SA* 179). For Jacob's story, like his father Isaac's, overturns the usual law of primogeniture. The younger son wrests the birthright from the elder son, Isaac from Ishmael, Jacob from Esau, Joseph from Reuben. "The firstborn very often seem to be losers in Genesis by the very condition of their birth . . .

while an inscrutable, unpredictable principle of election other than the 'natural' one works itself out" (Alter 6). Hagar, like the God of Abraham, would reverse the order of nature. The whole story of the Covenant celebrates such a reversal. Hagar can't understand it. John is the younger son. He should be chosen. She herself has done her best to reject nature, the mother, mortality. But her awful strength achieves nothing. She cannot change fate or nature. Hagar is Hagar, her second son, Ishmael. The story of the Covenant remains an enigma to her, a tale told in a foreign language.

Yet in the very moment she stops willing it, the story is given to her. Her first son reveals himself as Jacob, the child of the Promise. When she lets down her stony mask and gives in to nature, she is no longer blinded by fear:

> "I'm frightened. Marvin, I'm so frightened. . . ."
> What possessed me? I think it's the first time in my life I've ever said such a thing. Shameful. . . .
> I stare at him. Then, quite unexpectedly, he reaches for my hand and holds it tightly.
> Now it seems to me he is truly Jacob, gripping with all his strength, and bargaining. *I will not let thee go, except thou bless me*. And I see I am thus strangely cast, and perhaps have been so from the beginning, and can only release myself by releasing him. (*SA* 303-04)

The story inherited from her ancestors does not constrain her after all. It prompts her to tell a lie to Marvin. But her new story is not in fact "a lie, for it was spoken at least and at last with what may perhaps be a kind of love" (*SA* 307). It is one of only two moments in her life when she is "truly free." The other is when she can laugh at appearance—most of all her own—with Sandra Wong, the "celestial, as we used to call them" (*SA* 286). "Come ye before Him and rejoice" (*SA* 292), her minister had sung for her in a language she could understand. The joyous Hagar has become her own angel.

"Can angels faint?" she prefaces her final struggle with the Father. "*Our Father*—no. I want no part of that. All I can think is—*Bless me or not, Lord, just as You please, for I'll not beg*" (*SA* 307). "The special triumph of will wrought by Laurence in Hagar's characterization is thus a guarantee that readers will remember Hagar not only for what she chose, but for what she rejected" (Jeffrey 97). Unless, of course, Hagar is not rejecting, but wrestling. As angels are wont to do. For her whole story has inverted the Biblical one. Her father, not her husband, sent her into exile; her son sought her blessing, not his father's; she has evaded all her life the claim of the mother, not of the Father God. So the final problem of the "angel" is to find her place in a story which is no longer patriarchal.

"I wrest from her the glass, full of water to be had for the taking. I hold it in my own hands. There. There" (*SA* 308). It is a breathtaking moment in a lifelong struggle. For the angel herself is transformed into Jacob. Her desperate quest for metamorphosis is rewarded at last. But only when she has faced up fully to her past, like Jacob wrestling with the angel the night before he confronts his brother Esau:

> And he said, I will not let thee go, except thou bless me.
>
> And he said unto him, What is thy name? And he said, Jacob.
>
> And he said, Thy name shall be called no more Jacob, but Israel: for as a prince hast thou power with God and with men, and has prevailed . . .
>
> And Jacob called the name of the place Peniel: for I have seen God face to face, and my life is preserved.
>
> (*AV*, Gen. xxxii: 26-28, 30)

"Jacob is a man who sleeps on stones, speaks in stones, wrestles with stones, contending with the hard unyielding nature of things" (Alter 55). Hagar likewise never stops struggling against the unyielding nature of things. But the angel with whom "Jacob" wrestles is the nurse, the nurturer, the rejected mother; the angel does not come from the Father's heaven but from the depths of the heroine's maternal nature. The Covenant itself must be rewritten; old names must be changed to express the new meaning.

"Jacob, *Ya'aqov*, whose name . . . could be construed as 'he will deceive' " (Alter 43), is the better name for the woman who discovers her truth in "a lie." The truth is that her first-born is her true child, as the second son knows. " 'You always bet on the wrong horse,' John said gently. 'Marv was your boy, but you never saw that, did you?' " (*SA* 237). The moment she acknowledges as much, the rest of the old tale is given to her. Quite naturally. For the mysterious principle of election gives way to nature itself. Hagar's story does subvert Genesis after all. But only when she quits trying.

"*There. There.*" At the end, the "female Jacob" speaks the language she has learned from her daughter-in-law Doris: "She only repeats over and over the mother-word. 'There, there. There, there' " (*SA* 66). After she accepts her own maternity, "Jacob" blesses herself. Quite rightfully. In the end, she needs to mother herself. To accept her identity with the dead mother. The stone angel is made flesh.

"*And then—*" (*SA* 308). The novel ends. Open-endedly. In a way that *The Diviners* does not. Though both are stories about story and story-telling, the family likeness gives way to individual difference. For *The Diviners* rests in conclusions that Hagar has learned to reject. Morag's "totally invented memories" (*Div* 10) belong to a species of art which wants its independence from nature. Like Abraham's God, Morag seeks to make herself the pattern of an artificial order. She invents herself out of the junkyard of memory, willing herself to be a new creature. Yet, paradoxically, she cannot transform herself in the telling.

On the other hand, Hagar has had enough of the patriarchal story of self-invention. To the end, she will not say *Our Father*. To do so would deny the logic of her whole story. But she does say yes at last to something beyond her own making. She consents to death. To the Mother. To Nature.

Hagar's story restores to health what the post-modernists say they are sick of: "the concept of *tragic* feeling. . . . Saying Yes to life even in its strangest and hardest problems, the will to life rejoicing over its own inexhaustibility even in the very sacrifice of its highest types. . . . *Not* in order to be liberated from terror and pity, not in order to purge oneself of a dangerous affect by its vehement discharge—Aristotle understood it that way—but in order to be *oneself* the eternal joy of becoming, beyond all terror and pity—that which included even joy in destroying" (Nietzsche 562-63).

Gaiety transfiguring all that dread.

The stone angel cracks. Crumbles. Art itself gives way to seasonal process. But in the midst of ruin, the story-teller embraces her demon Fear. And finds the same release as those serene figures in "Lapis Lazuli":

> One asks for mournful melodies;
> Accomplished fingers begin to play.
> Their eyes mid many wrinkles, their eyes,
> Their ancient, glittering eyes, are gay. (Yeats 160)

Works Consulted

Alter, Robert. *The Art of Biblical Narrative*. New York: Basic Books, 1981.

Coldwell, Joan. "Hagar as Meg Merrilies, the Homeless Gypsy." *Journal of Canadian Fiction* 27 (1980): 92-100.

Davidson, Cathy N. "Past and Perspective in Margaret Laurence's

The Stone Angel." *American Review of Canadian Studies* 8 (1978): 61-69.

Gom, Leona M. "Laurence and the Use of Memory." *Canadian Literature* 71 (1976): 48-58.

Jeffrey, David L. "Biblical Hermeneutics and Family History in Contemporary Canadian Fiction: Wiebe and Laurence." *Mosaic* 11 (Spring 1978): 87-106.

Kertzer, Jon M. "*The Stone Angel*: Time and Responsibility." *Dalhousie Review* 54 (1974): 499-509.

Laurence, Margaret. *The Diviners*. 1974. Toronto: McClelland and Stewart, 1986.

———. *The Stone Angel*. 1964. Toronto: McClelland and Stewart, 1968.

Nietzsche, Friedrich. "Twilight of the Idols." *The Portable Nietzsche*. Trans. Walter Kaufmann. New York: Viking Press, 1954.

Thomas, Clara. *The Manawaka World of Margaret Laurence*. 1975. Toronto: McClelland and Stewart, 1976.

Thompson, Anne. "The Wilderness of Pride: Form and Image in *The Stone Angel*." *Journal of Canadian Fiction* 15 (1975): 95-110.

Yeats, W.B. "Lapis Lazuli." *Selected Poems and Two Plays*. Ed. M.L. Rosenthal. New York: Collier, 1966.

Keith Louise Fulton
University of Manitoba
University of Winnipeg

Feminism and Humanism: Margaret Laurence and the "Crisis of the Imagination"

> No revolution has yet dared understand its artists. Perhaps the Feminist Revolution will.
> —Robin Morgan

I. Feminism and Humanism

TILLIE OLSEN WRITES, "*It was the denial of this endowment to live the whole of human life*, the confinement of woman to a sphere, that brought the Women's Rights movement into being in the last century—feminism born of humanism. . . ." She adds that the acceptance of "age-old constrictive definitions of woman at a time when they are less true than ever to the realities of most women's lives—and need not be true at all—remains a complex problem for women writing in our time" (63). In her fiction Margaret Laurence explores the constricting definitions of women and dramatizes the ways that a woman's voice becomes a means to her self-realization. Yet our description of Laurence's work is often phrased in terms historically associated with these same definitions. Our understanding of Laurence, and of ourselves if we are to survive, requires more careful naming.

In a movement towards awareness and social justice, feminism addresses the failures and limits of humanism. As such it is a perspective on the present that is developed through an understanding of women's realities in the past and a vision of the future. The focus and concern of humanism has always been on the knowledge of man; in this knowledge man is the measure of humanity, and as Simone de Beauvoir has described, woman is 'other.' Humanism has shown us thoughts and images of men where women were shadowy figures in the background, supplying—as Susan Groag Bell observes—the nurturance of all people and occasionally the inspiration of a few. Feminism does not seek to reverse these roles or the imbalance of power, but to create a perspective allowing us to see the realities of women's lives that have been invisible to us. In a familiar example of field reversal, the white negative space surrounding a single black urn can, with a shift of perspective, become the silhouettes of two people. Consider this urn as the classical symbol, the urn of life, the single container of universal humanity, the mankind which humanist thought has given us; now reverse the field and consider the two blank oppositely gendered faces that single focus has disguised: woman and man. The work of Margaret Laurence aided me to discover that shift of perspective, to see that in place of one dark symbol for humanity, two luminous figures faced each other. Her work taught me not only that it was possible to see two in the place of one, but that it was absolutely necessary, if I was to see clearly at all.

Vision is a metaphor Laurence uses recurrently, from the sightless eyes of the Stone Angel to the anguished Morag in *The Diviners*: "The feeling of being separated from herself increases. . . . How can she write if she goes blind inside?" (263). Laurence's novels, about how these and other women recover their vision, offer a shift in perspective far more complex than the example of field reversal I have used. This example is helpful, however, because it reminds us of the multiple and simultaneous visions we have; how even when we have seen the two unknown figures instead of the single urn, that urn remains the dominant image always present at the centre yet given definition equally by each of the two figures. Basic changes in the forms of our perceptions are as rare as changes in the forms of writing. Margaret Laurence writes that with "the occasional rare genius" in writing, "truly new forms are evolved, and . . . the face of the language is changed" (Gadgetry 80). In Laurence's novels, the face we see is a woman's face—and that changes everything.

The tone of Margaret Laurence's voice in her novels has been described as "deeply humanistic," although the reviewer is aware of Laurence's concern with "female subjectivity and what being the subject of one's own story means" (Howells 39). The adjective, however intended, obscures the change in the face of language that Laurence creates and explores, and loses her work in the high sounding abstractions and male orientation of humanism. Laurence herself is sometimes apologetic in acknowledging a focus on women:

> I'm 90% in agreement with Women's Lib. But I think we have to be careful here . . . for instance, I don't think enough attention has been paid to the problems men have and are going to have increasingly because of the changes taking place in women. Men have to be re-educated with the minimum of damage to them. These are our husbands, our sons, our lovers . . . we can't live without them, and we can't go to war against them. The change must liberate them as well. (Atwood 23)

By focussing on men, Laurence obscures the realities of women's oppression, so that the liberation of women sounds like privilege, where women's well-being damages men's, where her empowerment makes him powerless. Laurence's own novels disprove this idea.

The persistence of the fear of reversal, however, is not surprising. Even without scholarship into the historical formation and maintenance of gendered roles for women and men, many of us know from our own experiences that men's privilege has been at the expense of women. Historically, in each revolution liberating mankind, men's freedoms have been gained partially through women's subordination. In her article "Did Women Have a Renaissance?" Joan Kelly discusses the upsurge of humanist learning, taking "the emancipation of women as a vantage point," and she discovers that "events that further the historical development of men, liberating them from natural, social, or ideological constraints, have quite different, even opposite, effects upon women" (139). She concludes, "Renaissance ideas on love and manners, more classical than medieval, and almost exclusively a male product, expressed this new subordination of women to the interests of husbands and male-dominated kin groups and served to justify the removal of women from an 'unladylike' position of power and erotic independence" (161). Kelly identifies the humanistic education of the Renaissance noblewoman as one of the reasons she lost power to create culture and the corresponding power to shape society: "Adopting the universalistic outlook of their humanist teachers, the noblewomen of Renaissance Italy seem to have lost all consciousness of their particular interests as women . . ." (152).

Regaining consciousness of our particular interests as women is central to feminism and a major theme in Laurence's writing. The struggle at the heart of women's liberation, however, is not a struggle for privilege, but for equality and self-determination. It is a struggle we share with all humans; that said, it does not follow that women can achieve equality and self-determination by using the language of humanism. We do not yet understand how completely this historical movement has enshrined hierarchy, privilege, and the corresponding oppressions in every aspect of our lives, our society and our knowledge. And yet, amazingly, humanism is widely regarded as egalitarian, while feminism is frequently held to be ideological with all the implications of narrow polemics. Laurence herself separates her feminist sympathies from her sense of her writing:

> I have not taken an active or direct part in the women's movement, just as I have not taken an active or direct part in any party politics, simply because my work resides in my fiction, which must always feel easy with paradox and accommodate contradictions, and which must, if anything, proclaim the human individual, unique and irreplaceable and the human spirit, amazingly strong and yet in need of strength and grace. (Ivory 258)

Yet art is part of the Women's Movement, and Laurence's writing is part of that art.

II. A Woman's Voice

In each of Laurence's Manawaka novels, the central human individual proclaimed is female, and the activity explored in all its paradox and contradiction is the growth of her consciousness. What makes Laurence's approach to paradox and contradiction feminist is, first, that the human individual *is* female and, second, that her problems come not only from her roles in the world, but also from the way her consciousness has been shaped by that world. Her growth is achieved and charted in the reclamation and discovery of her own voice.

Laurence's dramatization of the writer Morag in *The Diviners* shows that she understands the significance a woman's voice has to her ability to author her own life. Like the women who receive a humanist education, Morag has learned male cultural authority. The paternalistic man she marries and ultimately must leave is a professor of English and a humanist. Brooke reads Morag's first book about a young writer and observes that she

> ". . . is non-verbal, that is she talks a lot, but she can't communicate very well."

Morag responds,

> "I know that. I know. That was part of the problem."
> "I also wonder," Brooke says, flicking pages, "if the main character—Lilac—expresses anything which we haven't known before?" (246)

Morag's response is silent, but determined;

> "No. She doesn't. But *she* says it. That is what is different." (246)

Is human freedom, when it is sought and articulated by a woman, different from what we have "known before"? When a woman's freedom is limited, not because she is human, but because she is a woman, then yes. As male, husband, and professor, Brooke's hegemonic 'we' does not include Morag and never has, as Laurence clearly knows. Between Morag of *The Diviners* and Hagar of *The Stone Angel* are the voices of Rachel, Stacey, and Vanessa. Each of these discovers the stories and mythologies that have deceived them. Included in these are the stories each has constructed herself as she tries to make sense of her experience within the structures she has learned.

Feminism like fiction must accommodate the paradox and contradictions of our experience within patriarchal society. "Feminist criticism grew out of a Women's Liberation movement which took seriously the work of critiquing all of culture, from beauty pageants to university texts, in terms of its reflection of, and impact on, women's lives" (Rich 87). While the critique began with the more obviously sexist institutions, it also addresses the cultural production of women. We know that women work, have always worked. Where does our energy go? How do we contribute to the internal and external structures that oppress us? What is the impact on women of our support for a scholarship evolved along humanist lines? What are our experiences? Adrienne Rich defines feminist literary criticism as "a criticism which is consciously involved in a movement for women's liberation—indeed, a revolutionary movement" (87-88). This is the criticism we need if we are to understand our artists. Barbara Smith writes in her essay, "Toward a Black Feminist Criticism":

> Before the advent of specifically feminist criticism in this decade, books by white women . . . were not clearly perceived as the cultural manifestation of an oppressed people. It took the surfacing of the second wave of the North American feminist movement to expose the fact that these works contain a stunningly accurate record of the impact of patriarchal values and practice upon the lives of women and more significantly that literature by white women provides essential insights into female experience." (154)

It is not so paradoxical that the literature of relatively privileged white women is a record of cultural oppression, particularly when we look at how that literature answers questions we have raised.

Laurence addresses these questions in her prose and in her fiction: "I had had to abandon every *ism* except individualism and even that seemed a little creaky until the last syllable finally vanished of itself, leaving me ismless, which was just as well" (Ten 30). This was in 1962 after she had completed the first draft of *The Stone Angel*, a book that makes clear that although the individual—like Hagar—may prefer to live outside ideology, the structures of our world *are* ideological and to choose not to see them is to choose to be blind. The questions of women's experiences and patriarchal culture that Laurence poses through the individual Hagar come out of her African experiences and writings and what she had come to understand of tribalism, "an inheritance of us all" (Ten 31). That tribalism is to the good "if seen as the bond which an individual feels" (Ten 31) with roots, ancestors and background. While it may or may not be stultifying personally, that is a problem for each of us. But "where tribalism becomes . . . frighteningly dangerous is where the tribe . . . is seen as 'the people', the human beings, and the others, the un-tribe, are seen as sub-human." Then tribalism is everyone's problem (Ten 31).

Tribalism is a reality in Manawaka. There are many "un-tribes" in that hierarchical community: the poor, the Métis, the Natives. There is also another "un-tribe," however, whose existence even as an "un-tribe" is denied: women, Simone de Beauvoir's 'other'. Hagar Currie, daughter of Jason Currie, shares experiences with No-Name Lottie, the illegitimate daughter of an unnamed woman who dies young. Hagar hears Lottie's mother reject Jason's advances; Hagar's son dies with Lottie's daughter in an act of drunken despair brought on by a scheme for respectability conspired in by both Hagar and Lottie. She and Lottie, like John's observation of his father and grandfather, Bram Shipley and Jason Currie, "are only different sides of the same coin, anyway . . ." (184). Bram Shipley's uncouth poverty is defined by Jason Currie's manners and propertied industry just as Lottie's illegitimacy is defined by Hagar's respectability. While these characters do not understand that their identities are shaped by the social roles they fulfill, the reader does. Hagar is as dependent on male controlled respectability as Lottie is—and suffers at least as much from her 'privilege' as Lottie does from her oppression. This may be one of the paradoxes feminist readers must address.

Adrienne Rich writes that "all privilege is ignorant at the core" (227). Hagar's terrible darkness is that the ignorance that enslaves her to her so-called privilege alienates her from herself, from those she loves, and even from her ability to love. To deal with that ignorance is to risk losing status, and in case we're inclined to cluck our tongues at Hagar's "pride," let's remember that her "status" is directly linked to her survival. She is dependent on her father until she forfeits that support for her sexual need for Bram, and she is dependent on her husband (where she can raise money of her own only by peddling eggs!) until she forfeits her love of his body in an attempt to gain some control over her own; she leaves her independence when age and illness and death take it from her.

Recalling now my first reading of this book years ago, I am reminded of Hagar's coming on her own note in the margins of poems, "scribbled there by a nincompoop who'd borne my Christian name" (126). Though I know that this book touched me and helped me, if I had been asked then what I thought, I might have responded with what I had learned about first-person narrators, focussing on the faulty record Hagar gives of her faulty relationships to others and to herself. Now I see not the spitefulness of an old, selfish woman, but the pain and terrible anger of a woman betrayed by age, her experiences, her bowels, her tears—but shown by Laurence to be throughout betrayed by false stories, the false naming, of everything from manners, to morals, to love, to her own body. In *The Stone Angel*, Laurence dramatizes what a humanist critic might call life's betrayal of human passions, but she dramatizes the specific circumstances of these betrayals. Hagar's desire to rejoice, her passion, is betrayed by learned conventions of what it means to be female.

The first betrayal in *The Stone Angel* is usually cited as Hagar's failure of others and not as her own betrayal by the expectations of her culture. As a girl Hagar refuses to put on her dead mother's old plaid shawl and to hold and comfort her dying brother Dan by letting him believe he is in his mother's arms. Hagar faults herself for being "unable to do it, unable to bend enough" (25). Matt, her oldest brother, is able to do what Hagar cannot; while his actions speak for his compassion, his risks are much less than hers. He might be called effeminate for his action, but she is being called on to *be* her mother. Remember—her mother *died* for being her mother. Hagar's fear of this identity of mother and death is shown in her own first labour when she is convinced that she will die in childbirth. Mothering—as desire, need, guilt, crime and punishment—is explored in Hagar as in Laurence's other characters: Rachel in *A Jest of God*, Stacey in *The Fire-Dwellers* and Morag in *The Diviners*. In each case the woman is alone—"special" in privilege or isolated in humiliation. Laurence herself acknowledges she felt "enormous guilt about taking time for writing away from my family" (Atwood 23).

III. Survival

Laurence writes that she had supposed her theme in *The Stone Angel* was freedom—as it had been in her African fiction, but learned that it was survival, "the attempt of the personality to survive with some dignity" (Ten 33-34). Nine years later, Laurence discusses the two themes together as she considers her character Morag, "who is able to assimilate her past and to accept herself as a strong and independent woman, able to love and to create" (Ivory 258-59). For feminists, the goal of women's freedom is coupled with a concern for women's survival and an understanding of the real conditions of our lives. Laurence writes:

> The themes of freedom and survival relate both to the social/external world and to the spiritual/inner one, and they are themes which I see as both political and religious. If freedom is, in part, the ability to act out of one's own self-definition, with some confidence and with compassion, uncompelled by fear or by the authority of others, it is also a celebration of life and of the mystery at life's core. (Ivory 259)

Freedom, acting out of "one's own self-definition," is denied to women; in fact, the history of women parallels "the history of imperialism, of being defined in others' terms, not our own" (Ivory 257). Laurence explains her understanding of the colonial mentality with its "deep anger and resentment at betrayal and selfbetrayal" (Ivory 257) and relates the development of her feelings to her

> growing awareness of the dilemma and powerlessness of women, the tendency of women to accept male definition of ourselves, to be self-deprecating and uncertain, and to rage inwardly. (Ivory 258)

She makes clear that the survival she has in mind is "not mere physical survival, but a survival of the spirit, with human dignity and the ability to give and receive love" (Ivory 258).

While these terms could apply to a woman or to a man, to understand Laurence's work as a new humanism is to participate in the ignorance that is at the core of privilege, to ignore the power relationships that make patriarchy work. Gloria Steinem writes that women's acting "together with other women and becoming self-identified, female-identified, is a very long and inevitable part of gaining the power to reach a humanistic society in which we can integrate women and men, black and white as individual, equally powerful human beings . . ." (267). Such a humanistic society is only made more distant by the denial of women's experiences with social inequality, for that denial disempowers us, as any woman who has been victimized and then silenced or disbelieved can attest to.

Of course, it is not women alone who are colonized, taught to become a self-hating people, unsure of our voices, of our own experiences. Laurence's analysis comes from her understanding of African and Canadian experiences. In her fiction she shows that age, race and class, like gender, are also bases of oppression. In *The Diviners*, Laurence dramatizes the voices and experiences of Morag, the orphan taken in by the garbage collector Christie Logan and his gigantically fat wife Princess, of Lazarus Tonnerre whose father had fought with Riel at Batoche, of Skinner Tonnerre, of Skinner and Morag's daughter Pique, named for her dead aunt Piquette. As we see, however, in the stories of Piquette Tonnerre in "The Loons" and of Valentine from *The Fire-Dwellers*, the women who suffer race and class oppression are also further discriminated against because they are women. Piquette dies in a fire in the old shack where she retreats with her two children, and Valentine when Stacey meets her in Vancouver is dying of cancer while she survives as a hooker.

IV. Speaking Our Release and the Crisis of the Imagination

When I first thought of this paper on feminism and humanism and the problem of false naming, two passages from Laurence's work came to mind, passages that are deeply and disturbingly connected. The first comes from the beginning of *The Fire-Dwellers*, when Stacey, a mother of four, goes to bed with her husband Mac. He is angry at her for going to their son Duncan who is crying in his nightmare, for Mac can't bear the thought of his son's "insufficient masculinity. He wonders what will happen when they leave home, what unnatural flowering" (22). Stacey makes peace, promising to try not to baby the boy: "I will. Honestly. —I will. I will anything . . . I will promise anything, for peace. Then I'll curse myself for it, and I'll curse you, too. Oh Mac" (24). The self-denial makes her "tired" sexually just when Mac isn't; she tries to hide her feelings and touches him, as she says, "sirenly." Her choice of words is significant. The Sirens, as we know, sing so beautifully that passing sailors are overcome with longing, lured to the rocks and destroyed. Their story comes to us from the classical male writings at the core of humanism: a story Stacey knows too from her evening courses at the university, where she is also taught that she hasn't got "quite the right slant on Clytemnestra . . . [that] she murdered her husband" (27). While Stacey's choice of the word 'sirenly' might suggest self-knowledge and judgement, it comes from a classical, misogynist perspective that Stacey rejects—even in class: to her, "the king sacrificed their youngest daughter for success in war" (27). What happens to Stacey in bed is an image of her dilemma:

> When he is inside her, he puts his hands on her neck, as he sometimes does unpredictably. He presses down deeply on her collarbone.
>
> Mac   please
>
> That can hurt you   not that much   that's not much. Say it doesn't hurt.
>
> It hurts.
>
> It can't. Not even this much. Say it doesn't hurt.
>
> It doesn't hurt.
>
> He comes then, and goes to sleep. (24)

Later in the novel, when Mac has believed his friend Buckle's claim to having had sex with Stacey, Stacey finds a more accurate name for their activity:

> That night in bed he makes hate with her, his hands clenched around her collarbones and on her throat until she is able to bring herself to speak the release. It doesn't hurt. You can't hurt me. (144)

Speaking the release is a terrible parody of the consciousness raising that women have used to free ourselves by naming our experiences. For Stacey to free herself—not in Laurence's terms of self-definition—but from the choking hands of her husband, she must deny her own feelings, not implicitly, but in words: "It doesn't hurt." She must participate in the false naming of her reality.

The second passage comes from Laurence's discussion in the film *Speaking Our Peace*:

> "One very great problem in the nuclear arms race is what I would call a crisis of the imagination. It seems to me that a lot of the world's leaders . . . don't seem to have any imagination. They can talk about megadeath, they can talk about two hundred million people being

> killed just like that, and it doesn't seem to enter their consciousness that these are real live human beings that they're talking about—our children, real people, who in a nuclear holocaust would die horribly."

In a "crisis of the imagination" we use words that are emptied of human feeling; 'megadeath' has meaning—strategically, politically, economically—but the meaning does not connect to "real live human beings . . . who would die horribly." In a "crisis of the imagination" we do not extend the meaning of a word beyond a closed circle of its verbal context. The technique of partitioning meaning from experience is familiar to politicians, business people, bureaucrats, and professors. In contrast, Laurence feels her character's realities and acknowledges that a character is one of her "voices and selves" (Time 156). What is missing in a "crisis of the imagination" is the ability "to feel the reality of others" and that lack "enables people to become so brutalized that they are able to torture and murder their fellow human beings . . ." (*Speaking*). What is missing is the intelligent quality of empathy.

The "crisis of the imagination" does not happen all of a sudden to leaders once they gain power to make decisions about nuclear arms. The crisis begins in the home. Stacey and Mac live in what Laurence calls a "world on fire," a post-nuclear world that is our own. Stacey is one of Laurence's selves and some of her experiences are Laurence's own: for example, the child's bringing home from school a form for parents to list next of kin in the event of a nuclear disaster. Laurence brings the nameless realities of our fear and anger into the articulated world of the novel. Stacey writes on the child's form: "Name: God. Address: Heaven" (56), but her son, furious with embarrassment, takes the form to Mac, and Stacey, reproved, writes: "Matthew MacAindra (grandfather), Apartment 21, 704 Ballantyne Road"—God the father. Later we learn that Matthew, Mac's Presbyterian father, "like Moses, bearing in his eyes the letter of the Law" (115), carries the guilt for being too hard on Mac when he was a boy. Mac, in turn, cannot show love for his son and holds him for the first time after his near drowning at age seven. Like the begats in Genesis, the seed of guilt and judgement is borne on wordlessly. Stacey acknowledges that Mac's gruff silence is a kind of language—and one she uses too sometimes (266). When she insists that the old and blind Matthew come to live with them and hears his admission of guilt, she thinks, "Why did I ever once feel that to tell the truth the whole truth and nothing but the truth would be a relief? It would be dynamite, that's all it would be. It would set the house on fire" (253). But there are costs to lies, silence, misnaming and evasion.

Laurence closes *The Fire-Dwellers* by solving for the moment the "crisis of the imagination" in the manner of comedy: a happy marriage after all. Stacey and Mac talk to each other almost truthfully and make love compassionately, "gently, as though consoling one another for everything that neither of them can help nor alter" (276). I am reminded of Jane Austen's wise, satiric and bitter words: "Seldom, very seldom, does complete truth belong to any human disclosure; seldom can it happen that something is not a little disguised, or a little mistaken; but where, as in this case, though the conduct is mistaken, the feelings are not, it may not be very material" (297).

In the world of *The Fire-Dwellers*, however, both conduct and feelings are repeatedly mistaken and the consequences are material for the individual and for humanity. Stacey's neighbour Tess tries to commit suicide—no surprise to Katie, Stacey's teenage daughter: "Oh well, that's the usual gimmick, isn't it? . . . You never read the papers?" (244-45). Tess's despair and suicide attempt are not personal, but social. Early in the novel, Stacey senses her entrapment in the suburban buying parties:

> How strange if Bertha and Tess were thinking the same thing. We could unite. This could start an underground

> movement. The Bluejay Crescent Irregulars. I can see it all now. We're too damn complacent. No—we're not complacent one bit. We're just scared. (77)

They do not speak their release to each other, but mouth the lies: "it doesn't hurt."

Stacey tries to break out through education, but the university betrays her. Here we see the honesty and depth of Laurence's understanding, for Stacey is betrayed not just by the young male professor who cannot imagine Clytemnestra's rage for her sacrificed daughter but also by a woman professor teaching "Aspects of Contemporary Thought," who responds to Stacey's worry for the world by saying, "Pre-mourning is a form of self-indulgence" (9). Stacey does grow beyond "that aloof crystalline voice," for by the end of the novel she wonders "what it was that might have been meant by *Pre*" and considers a newspaper photograph:

> slash-eyed woman crouched on some temporarily unviolated steps in the far city, skull and bones outstanding under shriveled skin, holding the dead child, she not able to realize it is actually and unhelpably finished and yet knowing this is so. The woman's mouth open wide—a sound of unbearability but rendered in silence by the camera clicking. Only the zero mouth to be seen, noiselessly proclaiming the gone-early child. (250)

The woman's silencing through the photographic reporting, Clytemnestra's silencing through 2000 years of scholarly and mythological reporting, contribute to the fear Stacey feels when she acts or speaks on her own perceptions; with each step of self-assertion, she is terrified of a judgement that will fall not on her, but on her children.

Her fear, reinforced by patriarchal conditions and expectations for mothering, is not a delusion. In her work *The Creation of Patriarchy*, historian Gerda Lerner analyses how humans first learned to enslave other humans and points to the control maintained over the female through power exercised on her children, not just against them in the present, but in terms of her hopes for their future. Stacey does not know that other women share her sense of isolation and fear. She does not know about other women from history. When she comes on one of Tess's cosmetics named "Hetsheput" she asks what that means, and Tess answers that her husband had looked her up in a book:

> He came downstairs laughing like crazy and saying she was famous for her cruelty and she dressed as a man and married her stepson or some such relative and he hated her so much he had her name chiseled off all the monuments after she died. (167)

What a difference to Tess and to Stacey to have known about women's lives, not through cosmetics, male scholarship and vindictive husbands, but through voices spoken and interpreted by free women.

In their essay "But Is It Feminist Art?" Daphne Read, Rosemary Donegan and Liz Martin write:

> An important aspect of much feminist art is this process of naming the world from women's perspective—affirming the world as women experience it. When feminists name, they identify experiences and feelings in new and provocative ways—an essential process in consciousness-raising groups. It can be as straightforwardly significant as giving an experience a name—such as wife-beating—and making it visible, or as complex as treating artistically the experiences of groups not traditionally recognized in art: lesbians, Third World women, working women. Recognizing ourselves in art affirms our lives and struggles and helps us make connections with each other. (295-96)

Such art also helps us make connections between what we read and learn and what we experience. As Stacey begins to take action, the nature of truth changes for her from the dark certainties of repressed thought and creativity to the speculative, partial truths of expression and experience.

V. Changing the Face of Language

Although one act of mutually empowered conjugal embrace may point the direction of change, there are realities of this "world on fire" which it does not solve. The mother's mourning for her child in a nuclear age, Mac's coldness to Duncan, his homophobia, his choice of wife abuse to release his own need for power: these are not changed. Rosalie Bertel estimates that 16-17 million have died since 1945 from nuclear radiation. We don't have figures for the pain caused to sons by fearful fathers adhering to the patriarchal role of masculinity, for the pain and punishment dealt to women and men whose lives do not conform to heterosexist expectations. In Canada, the figures for wife-beating are one in ten, for wife abuse that includes emotional and economic abuse the figures are one in four. Until 1983 it was not even illegal in Canada for a man to rape the woman he was married to.

Laurence accepts the connection between fiction and social reality: "a novel can scarcely avoid being . . . a social commentary at a grassroots level" (Ivory 252) because our perceptions and interpretations are "formed by the communities in which we grow up" (Ivory 251). She explains that "writers of serious fiction are almost always . . . expressing their own times. This is true of historical fiction just as it is true of the writing of history itself. . . . In one way, fiction may be viewed as history, just as recorded history may be viewed as fiction" (Ivory 251-52). Feminist historians are alerting us to women's realities that are ignored or erased in historical accounts written by men. Who keeps the accounts and what these accounts say and do not say are all important to our understanding of both history and fiction. In each of Laurence's Manawaka novels, the record is of the voice—both inner and audible—of an individual woman with whom Laurence feels "a deep sense of connection . . . without a total identification" (Heart 2). From the beginning of her career as a writer, Laurence rejected omniscience—"the idea of the narrator's being able to whip in and out of the mind of more than one character at a time" (Gadgetry 81). What she communicates in each novel is the limited experience of an individual woman whose historical truth may be shared. From her we learn about the conditions of our present and of our past. From her we learn an empathetic, but not a universal, truth, for the limits and conditions of the protagonist's consciousness dramatize the limits of our own. Thus, Laurence can write that "If Hagar in *The Stone Angel* has any meaning, it is the same as that of an old woman anywhere, having to deal with the reality of dying. On the other hand, she is not an old woman anywhere. She is very much a person who belongs in the same kind of prairie Scots-Presbyterian background as I do . . ." (A Place 7).

We need to know about this woman. In her introduction to *The History of Prairie Women*, Candace Savage summarizes the movement of immigrant women to the prairies, to awareness of their collective realities, to organized political action that gained them the vote, to . . . what? "Then, just when it should have been time to reap the results, the movement withered like a frozen crop, leaving its leaders to wonder what had gone wrong" (8). The suppressed vocalization of the untribes, the unvoiced voices of the women Margaret Laurence creates, in her fully conscious attempt to explore and break out of colonization, help us to understand "what had gone wrong."

We also need to address the "crisis of the imagination" in the words we do use, for the failure to do so threatens not just our hopes for social justice, but for survival. By dramatizing in her narratives how the conditions of our lives are misnamed and how we are kept too fearful or proud to rename them, Laurence shows connections between the obscene words like megadeath and the denial of pain and empathy in individual lives. The imagination is a political faculty we cannot afford to ignore. Richness of imagination, the intelligent quality of empathy, is not the responsibility of the writer alone, however. The question here is not whether Laurence is a feminist writer, but whether we are feminist readers, able to recognize and understand the vision Laurence communicates and able to locate that vision within a historical tradition in which it makes sense. While that tradition may yet become a humanistic tradition, now—only 60 years after women became recognized politically as persons in Canada—is too soon. Laurence's work contributes to a feminist understanding of the historical failures of humanism to effect social justice; "Like love, like communication, like freedom, social justice must sometimes be defined in fiction by the lack of it" (Ivory 259). To recognize a "crisis of the imagination" in obscuring words is to enter the "struggle against lofty and privileged abstraction" (Rich 213), to learn our own minds and feelings, and to speak them. When women do this, we gain consciousness of our own particular interests as women. Changing the face of language is a first and necessary step in changing the realities women face.

Works Consulted

Atwood, Margaret. "Face to Face." 1974. *A Place to Stand On: Essays by and about Margaret Laurence*. Ed. George Woodcock. Edmonton: NeWest Press, 1983. 20-27.

Austen, Jane. *Emma*. Norton Critical Edition. Ed. Stephen M. Parrish. New York: W.W. Norton & Company, 1972.

Bell, Susan Groag. *Women: From the Greeks to the French Revolution*. Stanford: Stanford University Press, 1973.

Bertel, Rosalie. Interview. *Speaking Our Peace*. Dir. Bonnie Klein and Terry Nash. Studio D, National Film Board, 1987. See also,

Rosalie Bertel. *No Immediate Danger: Prognosis for a Radioactive Earth*. Toronto: The Women's Press, 1985.

Howells, Coral Ann. "Reading Margaret Laurence in England." *Canadian Women's Studies* 8.3 (1987): 38-42.

Kelly-Gadol, Joan. "Did Women Have a Renaissance?" *Becoming Visible: Women in European History*. Ed. Renate Bridenthal and Claudia Koonz. Boston: Houghton Mifflin Company, 1977. 137-64.

Laurence, Margaret. *The Diviners*. Toronto: Bantam Books, 1975.

__________. *The Fire-Dwellers*. Toronto: McClelland and Stewart-Bantam Limited, 1969.

__________. "Gadgetry or Growing: Form and Voice in the Novel." 1969. *A Place to Stand On: Essays by and about Margaret Laurence*. Ed. George Woodcock. Edmonton: NeWest Press, 1983. 80-89.

__________. *Heart of a Stranger*. Toronto: McClelland and Stewart-Bantam Limited, 1984.

__________. "Ivory Tower or Grassroots?: The Novelist as Socio-Political Being." 1978. *Canadian Novelists and the Novel*. Ed. Douglas Daymond and Leslie Monkman. Ottawa: Borealis Press, 1981. 251-59.

__________. Interview. *Speaking Our Peace*. Dir. Bonnie Klein and Terry Nash. Studio D, National Film Board, 1987.

__________. "A Statement of Faith." 1982. *A Place to Stand On: Essays by and about Margaret Laurence*. Ed. George Woodcock. Edmonton: NeWest Press, 1983. 56-60.

__________. *The Stone Angel*. Toronto: McClelland and Stewart Limited, 1964.

__________. "Ten Years' Sentences." 1969. *A Place to Stand On: Essays by and about Margaret Laurence*. Ed. George Woodcock. Edmonton: NeWest Press, 1983. 28-34.

__________. "Time and the Narrative Voice." 1972. *A Place to Stand On: Essays by and about Margaret Laurence*. Ed. George Woodcock. Edmonton: NeWest Press, 1983. 155-59.

Lerner, Gerda. *The Creation of Patriarchy*. Toronto: Oxford University Press, 1986.

MacLeod, Linda. *Battered But Not Beaten: Preventing Wife*

Battering in Canada. Ottawa: Canadian Advisory Council on the Status of Women, 1987.

Morgan, Robin. *Going Too Far: The Personal Chronicle of a Feminist*. New York: Random House, 1978.

Olsen, Tillie. *Silences*. New York: Dell Publishing Co. Inc., 1983.

Reed, Daphne with Rosemary Donegan and Liz Martin. "But Is It Feminist Art?" *Still Ain't Satisfied! Canadian Feminism Today*. Ed. Maureen Fitzgerald, Connie Guberman, Margie Wolfe. Toronto: The Women's Press, 1982. 287-99.

Rich, Adrienne. *Blood, Bread and Poetry. Selected Prose 1979-1985*. New York: W.W. Norton & Company, 1986.

Savage, Candace. Preface. *A Harvest Yet to Reap: A History of Prairie Women*. Ed. Linda Rasmussen, Lorna Rasmussen, Candace Savage, Anne Wheeler. Toronto: The Women's Press, 1976. 8-9.

Smith, Barbara. "Toward a Black Feminist Criticism." *All the Women Are White, All the Blacks Are Men, But Some of Us Are Brave: Black Women's Studies*. Ed. Gloria T. Hull, Patricia Bell Scott, and Barbara Smith. Old Westbury, New York: The Feminist Press, 1982. 157-75.

Steinem, Gloria. "The Politics of Supporting Lesbianism." *Our Right to Love: A Lesbian Resource Book*. Ed. Ginny Vida. Englewood Cliffs, New Jersey: Prentice Hall, 1978. 266-69.

Hans Hauge
University of Aarhus

The Novel Religion of Margaret Laurence

> . . . since Defoe the secularization of the novel has been continuous.
>
> —T.S. Eliot

> . . . do not impose on us any aesthetic rules which shall banish from the region of Art those old women.
>
> —George Eliot

> Imagine dying from a fractured skull delivered by a hysterical swallow. A novel death. In a novel, who'd believe it? Novel. Odd word.
>
> —Margaret Laurence

1. A Solid Lectern

WHEN MARGARET LAURENCE in 1982 gave an address to Emmanuel College called “A Statement of Faith,” she told her audience that she had “requested that a solid lectern be provided” because, as she continued, “I feel the need of something solid to lean on, physically, but also the need—not just now but every day—of something spiritual to lean on. This sustaining force is faith” (56). In “Face to Face” Margaret Atwood tells how Margaret Laurence, while staying at Trent University, used to say, “I can't give public speeches without a chair . . . if I stand up my knees knock together, I mean literally” (27). Laurence has written the well-known essay “A Place to Stand On,” the title of which comes from Al Purdy's poem. Religion and the past are places to stand on although the solidity of these entities may not be so apparent. By religion and the past, Laurence means the Scots-Presbyterian background which, she has related, was created by people like Hagar Shipley. Hagar, however, was created by Margaret Laurence.

The repeated use of the figure “a place to stand on” should be juxtaposed with Northrop Frye's observations that writers of the last decade write in a world which is “post-Canadian” and in which “sensibility is no longer dependent on a specific environment or even on sense experience itself” (*The Bush Garden* 249). It is my contention that Laurence knew and experienced what Frye says and that she therefore, in the absence of a specific environment, had to create one. That is to say, she created Hagar so that she and her readers would have a place to stand on. Literature was to re-place religion and the past. Fiction as a solid lectern. *The Diviners*, however, signals literature's failure to provide such places and therefore she voiced her need for solidity after *The Diviners* in non-literary or non-fictional terms. She did not “create” new heroines, but identified with characters like Helen Caldicott. Her example shows that we are not fitted to live in that modern world where time can only be conceived of as history and where all horizons are only our horizons, as George Grant says.

Laurence has made several statements of faith. She has proclaimed her belief as a writer and as a Christian in the social gospel and the word (Word). She has never doubted that the writer has a responsibility to write as truthfully as possible and she adheres faithfully to a mimetic theory of literature: "art mirrors and ponders the pain and joy of our experience as human beings" (Final Hour 195). Just as she herself was deeply rooted in religious faith, so her novels seem firmly grounded in extra-literary reality. The novelist Margaret Laurence and the novels of Margaret Laurence have and are places to stand on: "Writing . . . has to be set firmly in some soil" (Place 18), she claims in what sounds almost like an answer to Frye's words quoted above. She is little affected by that "Nietzscheanism" which D.J. Dooley thinks has affected Canadian literature (James 255) and which George Grant argues has affected modern life as a whole. Laurence's statements of faith are often at the same time religious, ethical, and literary.

The separation of morality, religion and aesthetics which one sometimes, and not without reason, tends to take for granted appears not to apply in her case. The writing of a novel and the creation of a character is a religious as well as a literary act. Both religion and literature share in pointing to the "mystery and wonder at the core of life" (Twigg 267). Yet to say "create," as I have done, may be somewhat misleading. The very young Morag loves Jesus, but not God, since He "is the one who decides which people have got to die, and when" (*Div* 77). Laurence does not act like God—more like Jesus?—when she "makes" a character. She did not "create" Hagar, but "the reverse seemed to be true," she reports; "the character of Hagar in *The Stone Angel* seemed almost to choose me" (Place 16). Being chosen by a character Laurence describes in religious terms. It is a sense of grace, or being possessed.

On the whole Laurence is a traditional realistic writer and on the whole this is the way she has been read and received. Her novels have invited a so-called environmentalist reading or at least a thematic one. Recent criticism, however, reflects the linguistic turn which has influenced almost all intellectual currents, Canadian literary criticism included. The shift in Laurence-criticism away from thematic and towards genuinely literary readings (I am thinking of such critics as Theo Dombrowski, Michel Fabre, W.H. New and Pierre Spriet) also has something to do with the appearance of *The Diviners*. That novel puts into question the mimetic assumptions that lie behind her previous novels. It can be characterized as self-reflexive and metafictional. In her "Face to Face" Atwood reports that Laurence, right after the publication of *The Diviners*, told her, "I don't think I'll ever write another novel" (27). Theo Dombrowski has said that in *The Diviners* Laurence "suggests the loss of her ability to articulate in fiction" (61).

Significantly enough, the majority of the statements that I have referred to were issued after 1974. *The Diviners*, it seems in retrospect, was in more than one sense the culmination of the fictional world of Manawaka. It is a symptom of the separation between faith and art and the disappearance of the religious sense from the novel, something Graham Greene identifies with the disappearance of the belief in the objective existence of external reality. It is true, though, that several of Laurence's most sympathetic readers have continued to read her "religiously." Clara Thomas reads *The Diviners* as a "homecoming novel" (Thomas 172), and William C. James as a "vision of transcendence." This is suggested to him by the ability of divining to "probe beneath the surfaces of things" (James 255).

As far as I can see it is impossible to decide if divining is finding a meaning behind the surface or projecting one into things. Is it finding sense or making it? Morag is clearly aware that she reads nature in an anthropomorphic way. She doesn't *find* the truth, she *constructs* it. *The Diviners* is much less grounded than Laurence's other novels and stories. It is, to use Frye's words again, much less, if at all, dependent upon a specific environment, and hence the impossibility of an "environmentalist" reading.

2. The Novel as Social Gospel

The Diviners is not directly my subject here. I go back in time to 1964 to *The Stone Angel*. The major difference between *The Diviners* and *The Stone Angel* is that in the former Laurence is preoccupied with epistemological problems (the relation between fiction and fact, world and word, past and present), but in the latter she deals with ethical problems. There are no reflections in *The Stone Angel* about the validity of statements about the past nor about the relation between memory and imagination.

Hagar's memories are in chronological order, and neither Hagar nor Laurence have doubts similar to Morag Gunn's. Morag puts her snapshots and pictures into a chronological order although she realizes that by doing so she acts "as though there really were any chronological order, or *any order at all*, if it came to that" (*Div* 6, my emphasis). It is true that after having written *The Stone Angel* Laurence did reflect on the way she had depicted Hagar's memories and used the flash-back technique. She realized that perhaps we do not remember in a chronological order at all:

> In some ways I would have liked Hagar's memories to be haphazard. But I felt that . . . the result of such a method would be to make the novel too confusing for the reader . . . one can say that the method diminishes the novel's resemblance to life. . . . (Gadgetry 83)

Order in the novel is there for the sake of the reader and not for the sake of realism. Realism in *The Stone Angel* is pragmatic rather than mimetic, although it is true that Laurence was convinced of the authenticity of Hagar's voice.

But what has this to do with religion? Laurence had quite an unorthodox view of God. According to her theology God loves disorder and hence the world was created disorderly. When we create, we impose order on a disorderly world. It is therefore a serious matter to diminish a novel's resemblance to life because it simultaneously diminishes its religious value. As a Protestant Laurence was easily familiar with a tension between art and religion, and it is this traditional tension which surfaces as a tension between art-as-order and religion-as-disorder. By appealing to the reader she redeems her novel; she feels justified in sacrificing the mimetic (and thereby the disorder). All the references to the Bible, the quotations from hymns and psalms, the quasi-theological discussions amongst the characters do not constitute the religious aspect of the novel. Neither do they contribute to the mimetic aspects of it. Mimesis seems to be a formal thing. A disorderly novel (like *The Diviners*?) is more religious than an ordered one.

A novel, then, should not mean but do. A novel's truth is what it does, and this concept of truth is Biblical. What does the novel then perform, rather than state? Firstly, it furnishes the reader with a place to stand on, and secondly it performs an ethical act. Let me discuss the former aspect first. *The Stone Angel* provides the (Canadian) reader with a solid ground. Laurence knew that in modernity all that is solid melts into air. It provides the reader with a place by rehabilitating Canada's Puritan past. *The Stone Angel* is a re-evaluation of nineteenth-century Protestantism. This may sound somewhat odd, for how can an old dying woman function as an ideal, a model, or a type? In what sense can Hagar be a symbol and a revaluation of the Puritan past?

Before answering, one should note that Laurence is not alone in a revaluation of the Protestant past. In Alan Twigg's interview with Dennis Lee in *For Openers* Lee says that "it's the older Methodist/Presbyterian tradition I've started to respect now. I mean the rectitude, the honesty and the sense that you lived an unadorned life . . . that old Wasp integrity, stultifying though it was, starts looking pretty valuable" (249). I should like to supplement this with a few remarks made by John Webster Grant about the collapse in very recent times of the nineteenth-century Christian programme for Canada. Towards the end of his essay John Webster Grant says:

> The vision of a Christian society, whether conceived as a replica of the old Christendom or as an anticipation of the promised millennium, has clearly lost its power to inspire. What foundations of national identity have we put in its place? I confess myself hard put to give a satisfying answer . . . I cannot see any possibility that we shall remain long in the transitional phase if rebellion against an oppressive religion that no longer oppresses and one of the clearest messages of the 1970's is that the dimension of meaning once provided by the churches is still very much in demand. (19)

If the churches cannot provide the dimension of meaning or a foundation, then perhaps the novel can. The novel as a new place to stand on. The novel as social gospel? Laurence is, one could say, a "novel" social gospeller. In 1983 she conceded that the social gospel "is no easier now than it ever was" (Final Hour 189). It is difficult because the social gospel has never been able to dissociate itself sufficiently from certain ideas such as the belief in progress and rationality and nationalism. In systematic terms the social gospel is the translation of religious tradition into purely ethical terms. Peter Berger describes it in this way: "To strive for justice, to be compassionate, to have concern for the poor or oppressed . . . all these need not have anything to do with any supernatural definition of reality" (114).

If we combine these remarks with what a realistic novel is, one can say that the remarks are equally true of the novel.

A novel need not have anything to do with any supernatural definition of reality, in fact it *cannot if it is to remain a novel.* If it has, it is a romance. There seems to be a perfect fit between an ethical version of Protestantism and the realistic novel. What is the content of the social gospel according to Laurence? "The new commandment of the man of Nazareth speaks very clearly. 'Thou shalt love thy neighbour as thyself' " (Final Hour 189). Is this new commandment, then, and can we say it as innocently as that, the "theme" of *The Stone Angel*?

3. *The Stone Angel* and the Ethics of Reading

I have claimed that *The Stone Angel* provides the (Canadian) reader with a new foundation, a place to stand on. Also, I propose to read it as an ethical novel or as an allegory of love. Once one has proposed to read the novel as a rehabilitation of Canada's Protestant past one encounters problems. Hagar is depicted as extremely critical of her own Scots-Presbyterian background which I have claimed is the novel's intention to revaluate. The character of Hagar moreover appears unsympathetic. She seems not only unlovable but incapable of loving. She is portrayed as being extraordinarily blind (a stone angel) and deaf to the commandment of The New Testament. Hagar's father's religion is shown to be pure ideology; a necessary tool with which to survive in a settlers' community. Hagar has seen through his religion, as the following quotation illustrates:

> Auntie Doll was always telling us that Father was a God-fearing man. I never for a moment believed it, of course. I couldn't imagine Father fearing anyone, God included, especially when he didn't even owe his existence to the Almighty. God may have created heaven and earth and the majority of people, but Father was a self-made man, as he himself had told us often enough. (*SA* 16-17)

While the Protestant Ethic is functional in Jason Currie's case, it is no longer so in Hagar's. She has taken over her father's version of Protestantism and secularized it even further by internalizing it. Since she is faced with no external wilderness to combat and survive in, she uses religion to survive in the inner wilderness. She *is* the wilderness, as Atwood has reminded us. Hymns and psalms no longer comfort her, though secular poetry does. She never attends church and mocks Doris for doing so. She is cruel towards the young minister who comes to comfort her. She hates being taken care of although she needs it. She never says what she means and she never means what she says.

How can one possibly identify with Hagar? How can she become a model? In what sense can the novel be a new foundation? Art should honour the past, Laurence says. But does she do so in *The Stone Angel*? First of all Laurence does not idealize the past. Being a realist, she describes the past as it really was. She did not yet put into question the novel's ability to represent the past truthfully. Though she has never said so it is my contention that her novels can be regarded as "typical" and that her characters are "types."

I use the word "type" the way it is used in the theory of socialist realism. Socialist realism and Laurence's version of social gospel realism are somewhat similar. A type, according to standard socialist realist theory, is at the same time an *Abbild* and a *Vorbild*. Hence a novel is typical, and the same goes for characters, if it is both mimetic (*Abbild*) and incarnates the principle of hope (*Vorbild*). Hagar and her cultural background are true representations of the past. Laurence talks about this in the following way: "She [Hagar] is very much a person who belongs in the same kind of prairie Scots-Presbyterian background as I do, and it was, of course, people like Hagar who created that background, *with all its flaws and strengths*" (Place 18, my emphasis).

The flaws of the past are evident enough. But what are its strengths? "In each novel there is some hope" (18), Laurence says—in my terminology, in each novel there is *Vorbild*. What one can learn from the past is the "determination to survive against whatever odds" (18). The past, as recreated in the novel, is there in order to strengthen us against, for instance, the nuclear threat. That is the way the Protestant past can still be functional. "Ours is a terrifying world" (Final Hour 188), Laurence reminds us. But the past has also helped Laurence the writer in another way. Just as Hagar's father is a self-made man, Laurence was a self-made writer, or at least she said she was. When she describes Hagar's father, she not only shows his flaws, but also his strengths. Indirectly she describes her own strengths as a writer. The passage about Hagar's father quoted above could also be read as a denial of influence. If Hagar created the past she also "created" her children, and the past as such "produced" all the characters who surround Hagar in the novel.

This brings me to what I think is "ethical" about the novel. The episode in the fish-cannery with Hagar and Murray F. Lees will provide a tentative answer to how the novel is an allegory of love. I would call the episode a rewriting of the parable of the Good Samaritan. We recall how the priest and the Levite passed by and how the Samaritan helped. The parable ends with the words "which now of these three, thinkest thou, was neighbour unto him that fell among the thieves? And he said, He that shewed mercy on him. Then said Jesus unto him, Go and do thou likewise" (KJV Luke 10: 36-37). *The Stone Angel* is the story of how Doris and Marvin and Mr. Troy and Mr. Lees and other characters have compassion on Hagar. She does not appear to deserve it; for the most part she has been incapable of love. Yet love is precisely what she achieves in the end. *The Stone Angel* shows how grace and love come even to the undeserving. In the final scene of the novel, Hagar, without really thinking about it, acts lovingly by helping the young girl in the hospital ward. Hagar becomes her neighbour.

I said above that the social gospel version of Protestantism has no need for what Berger calls supernatural definitions of reality. Likewise God cannot interfere in a realistic novel's universe. "In a novel, who'd believe it?" as Morag says. Where is God in *The Stone Angel*? There, as in the ethical sphere as such, we only meet God in the love other human beings show us, whether or not we deserve it. But this is not the end of the story. It is one thing to read about how fictional characters act ethically, act as "neighbours" and practise the new commandment. But the novel is not primarily "about" ethical acts. It is itself an ethical act. It literally says: Go and do thou likewise. Who is to do what? The reader. The novel succeeds if the reader begins to love Hagar. The act of reading becomes practising spontaneously the social gospel. Reading becomes an act of *caritas*.

4. A Place to Stand On—Again

I have argued that Margaret Laurence in *The Diviners* struggled with irresolvable epistemological problems. The act of representing history becomes problematic. It becomes impossible to tell if divining is finding or constructing a pattern. The epistemology of *The Diviners* can be characterized as scepticist. I am convinced that Laurence sensed this after having finished it. Literature could not be a place to stand on, unless one feels that fiction is solid ground. But that is precisely a "fiction."

I began by mentioning all the instances where Laurence expressed her need for a place to stand on. These statements pose an existential predicament. The development of her Manawaka novels goes from realism towards idealism. Once such idealism is *felt*, the ground begins to slip under one's feet. Physically and spiritually. Just as Wordsworth had the habit of grasping at "a wall or a tree to recall" himself from "this abyss of idealism to the reality" (Intimations Ode), Margaret Laurence needed solid lecterns. The act of writing and the act of reading, she saw, transform the world we thought we knew.

Works Consulted

Atwood, Margaret. "Face to Face." *A Place to Stand On: Essays by and about Margaret Laurence*. Ed. George Woodcock. Edmonton: NeWest Press, 1983. 20-28.

Berger, Peter L. *The Heretical Imperative*. New York: Anchor Press, 1979.

Dombrowski, Theo. "Word and Fact." *Canadian Literature* 80 (1979): 50-63.

Frye, Northrop. *The Bush Garden*. Toronto: Anansi, 1971.

Grant, John Webster. "Religion and the Quest for a National Identity." *Religion and Culture in Canada*. Ed. Peter Slater. CCSR, 1977. 7-23.

James, William C. "Religious Symbolism in Canadian Fiction." *Religion / Culture: Comparative Canadian Studies* ACS VII (1985).

Laurence, Margaret. *The Diviners*. Toronto: Bantam, 1982.

———. "Gadgetry or Growing: Form and Voice in the Novel." *A Place to Stand On: Essays by and about Margaret Laurence*. Ed. George Woodcock. Edmonton: NeWest Press, 1983. 80-89.

———. "My Final Hour." *Canadian Literature* 100 (1984): 187-97.

———. "A Place to Stand On." *A Place to Stand On: Essays by and about Margaret Laurence*. Ed. George Woodcock. Edmonton: NeWest Press, 1983. 15-20.

———. *The Stone Angel*. Toronto: McClelland & Stewart, 1984.

Thomas, Clara. *The Manawaka World of Margaret Laurence*. Toronto: McClelland & Stewart, 1976.

Twigg, Alan. *For Openers*. Madeira Park: Harbour Publishing, 1981.

Aritha van Herk
University of Calgary

The Eulalias of Spinsters and Undertakers

GOD'S GREATEST JEST is death. No, not death, the breath of mortality, but desire. No, not that we desire desire but that we dare not; castigate ourselves, censor all longing, appetite so inappropriate, so difficult to control, so demanding of its own fulfillment. Demands articulation, that desire, cries out for its own crying, speaks "the secrets of the core and marrow" (*JG* 17) in a voice that cannot be glossed, a voice ululating its own longing. Eulalia: a wordless cry, "the extremest coming" (Kroetsch 12), an/other singular fictional occurrence of the ultimate ululation. To give tongue to craving, the secret vowels of a secret language, wordless and yet articulate, with a coherence belonging only to itself. Give tongue to longing, to give tongue, to cry out intense delight/rapture, to call desire by its proper sound. The cries of love and the cries of longing are sisters, a kinship formed from the dream language that returns us to our bodies, unverbalized, postlexical (Marlatt 45). Eulalia: a woman's cry at the moment of orgasm. No other word—glossalalia, ululation, lallation—is enough.

A Jest of God gives novelistic tongue to a language that silences the body and to a language that speaks the body. Rachel Cameron's tongue gets in its own way, cleft/double-talk, gets in the way of its own desire. Rachel Cameron has the gift of tongues but cannot permit her tongue to emerge from the tomb of her mouth, "the tomb-like atmosphere of her extended childhood" (Ten Years 21), to unbury itself in a eulalic utterance. *A Jest of God* is her clamour, her shout, her whisper; it is, as George Bowering has stated, "the written word . . . as score for the tongue's workings" (161). That lallic propensity is made dilatory by Rachel's tongue-bridling mileau and past. Her tongue longs to utter her desire, to cry out in a rising ululation that she has stifled her entire life. *A Jest of God* undertakes to unearth Rachel's eulalia, long-buried: her glossalalia that cries out to God/father/lover/mortician for hearing.

Perhaps God's jest is the inevitable and ubiquitous self-censorship of silence and Rachel's final acceptance of her fool's role (

> I was always afraid that I might become a fool. Yet I could almost smile with some grotesque lightheadedness at that fool of a fear, that poor fear of fools, now that I really am one. (181)

) is a license to babel. (

> I will rage in my insomnia like a prophetess. . . . I may sing aloud, even in the dark. (202)

) God/the author's jest is the speaking of the novel itself, that outcry of words, a lallation of desire and consummation. But the novel as cry has been largely mis-heard, de-cried by a childish encoding of a word from one of those brutal nursery rhymes.

a spinster, a spinster, a spinster

Rachel's lallic longing is sadly mistaken by more than one critic, and the overweening chant with which her eulalia has been met is downright churlish.

> The sorrowful moan is constant. Visits to friends, her mother's bridge parties, her first sexual experience, the possibility of pregnancy, of cancer—all are given nearly equal emotional weight. Rachel is monolithic. Her character is carpeted wail-to-wail with her failures. Unable to be loveable, she is not loved; physically unattractive, socially inept, sexually fearful, one could imagine a psychiatrist giving up and uttering that famous line: "Let's face it, you *are* inferior."
>
> What is lacking—and even the difficult first person present tense technique, if properly used, could handle this fault—is objectivity, distance, irony. One simply gets tired of listening to Rachel taking pot-shots at herself. The reader, instead of identifying, finds himself (herself, too, I should think) silently shouting at her to get some eye-liner, save for a mink, strong-arm a man, kill her mother and stop bitching. (Harlow 190)

"Wail to wail." Harlow's review is more a judgement of Rachel Cameron's personal status than a reading of her voice. Harlow hears the cry, but mis-hears its desire. Rachel's eulalia is reduced by the archetypal male reader to a lack of objectivity, an absence of irony, a shortage of distance. This phallocentric ear would not hear eulalia if he were right on top of it, if he had actually managed to evoke that outcry. He hears another call.

> *a spinster, a spinster, a spinster*

Oh, that contemptuous and pitying scorn: a woman unmarried, past the age of marrying, unlikely to marry. Is all meaning connected to marriage, Rachel? The lack of a man the one true signifier, *spinster* torqued? (Daly). But a spinster is a woman whose occupation is to spin. To spin a yarn, a story:

Rachel, the dervishes spun too, in their ecstasy. And spiders, who spin, are renowned for their creativity and aggression. So Rachel, you spinster, you have been not mis-named but mis-heard, un-read.

As spinster, Rachel is elegized into a critical silence. "To Rachel we must . . . accord the shamefaced sympathy, partly based on condescension, that the legions of upright North American spinsters have always commanded" (Thomas 60). She is "a frustrated spinster schoolteacher" (Thomas 57).

a spinster, a spinster, a spinster

> *A Jest of God* portrays thirty-four year old Rachel Cameron desperately but ineffectively struggling against becoming a stereotype spinster schoolmarm, gaining a new lease on life through Nick Kazlik, becoming the butt of God the Jester, and awakening at last to an understanding of her own identity in a silent epiphany of self-affirmation. (Forman 85)

What is so wrong about these readings is their insistence on silence, when *A Jest of God* is the noisiest, most wildly eulalic outcry possible. It is the voicing of Rachel's discontent, the articulation of her desire. And while much is attributed to her "virginal doldrums" (Djwa 80), it might instead be the case that the entire novel is provoked by her vaginal doldrums; Rachel Cameron's glossalalia and ululation and lalliance is not only that of a woman grieving but of a woman crying out in the extremes of love, a woman daring to imagine such lovering. Her tumour is the cancer of longing and her desire itself a foreplay. Rachel imagines, cries for, the lover she will find in Nick Kazlik. (

> The trees are green walls, high and shielding, boughs of pine and tamarack, branches sweeping to earth, forming a thousand rooms among the fallen leaves. She is in the green-walled room, the boughs opening just enough to let the sun in, the moss hairy and soft on the

> earth. She cannot see his face clearly. His features are blurred as though his were a face seen through water. She sees only his body distinctly, his shoulders and arms deeply tanned, his belly flat and hard. He is wearing only tight-fitting jeans, and his swelling sex shows. She touches him there, and he trembles, absorbing her fingers' pressure. Then they are lying along one another, their skins slippery. His hands, his mouth are on the wet warm skin of her inner thighs. (18-19)

) The "rude, unmannerly" (13) act of love, even self-love, carries Rachel beyond voice for a short while; she enters the smooth silence of post-climax. Of course, it is not long before voice rises again, "his voice" (19), the voice of God/mortician/father/lover who arouses Rachel's own cry.

For the true undertaking of *A Jest of God* is the expression of Rachel's lust. Rachel desires/she lusts, and spinsterhood or no, she is the articulation of her own longing. The intensity of her desire for physical contact at any cost is enacted by her connection with James Doherty, the young student she is attracted to but cannot find the right voice/the right words for. Unable to elicit any verbal response from him, Rachel strikes him with her ruler, making his nose bleed. A physical response at least, a citation for Rachel's own outcry of blood. That outcry, in the first half of the novel, is largely imaginary, even though the existence of its imagining suggests Rachel's potential eulalia. (

> —When Egypt's queen received Antony, that book said, she used to fall upon him even before he had taken off his armour. Think of that—even before he'd taken off his armour. They used to have banquets with dozens there. Hundreds. Egyptian girls and Roman soldiers. Oasis melons, dusty grapes brought in the long ships from somewhere. Goblets shaped like cats, cats with listening ears, engraven in gold, not serpents or bulls, not Israel or Greece, only golden cats, cruelly knowledgeable as Egypt. They drank their wine from golden cats

> with seeing eyes. And when they'd drunk enough, they would copulate as openly as dogs, a sweet hot tangle of the smooth legs around the hard hairy thighs. The noise and sweat—the sound of their breath—the slaves looking on, having to stand itchingly immobile while they watched the warm squirming of those— (59)

) The voice here might be the sound of Rachel's breath, and these parenthetical scenes ululate past the governance of meaning, understandability, signification. They lallate Rachel's sexual desire and, in effect, gloss the tongue of the novel for us: a cry of anguish, a longing for touch.

Enclosed by these two parenthetical "fantasy" scenes is the famous glossalalia scene, where Rachel's ululation gets away on her and where her longing articulates itself publicly. Although the glossalalia scene is much noted as an obviously sexual moment, it is seldom actually glossed in eulalic terms. The erotics of glossalalia appear to be beyond Rachel, and yet her "*ecstatic utterances*" (27) go beyond all others; she has that eulalatory gift because she is practised in its outpouring, her whole life a honing to perfection of that anguished and enraptured cry. The tongues of men and angels clamour within the tabernacle of the body and the outer "*Tabernacle of the Risen and Reborn*" (29) is only a physical edifice to contain the obvious implication of rising and rebirth. Orgasm is a bodily cry shaped out of body experience, perhaps as close as humans can come to a truly religious experience: Rachel's orgasmic glossalalia is the verbal equivalent of her physical conjunction with Nick Kazlik.

Within the Tabernacle, Rachel is figuratively held by the bodies of the people around her, and that holding, its hot and close and shameful intimacy, is one of the causes for Rachel's sexual overwhelming, too much for her, she who has not been held, helps to pitch her toward the orgasm of voice that she experiences. At the same time, she images the tabernacle in terms of death. (

> The light seems distant and hazy, and the air colder than it can really be, and foetid with the smell of feet and damp coats. It's like some crypt, dead air and staleness, deadness, silence. (31)

) The crypt of the body needs to be opened and that first orifice is mouth; the voice. The preacher grows in stature, he is "all fervour" (34) and he holds his arms in the attitude of a lover. So that the hymns' keening, and Rachel's image of "the messengers of the apocalypse, the gaunt horsemen, the cloaked skeletons" (32) ride up from her imperative longing. (

> Let the Dionysian women rend themselves on the night hills and consume the god. (36)

) The moment the Dionysian image appears, we know that Rachel will speak, will voice her coming, her eulalic desire, there in that hot holding pour out her sexual longing. (

> Chattering, crying, ululating, the forbidden transformed cryptically to nonsense, dragged from the crypt, stolen and shouted, the shuddering of it, the fear, the breaking, the release, the grieving— (36)

) For of course orgasm is both relief and grief, *petit mort*, a recognition of mortality in the moment of greatest transcendence. Rachel's friend Calla talks about the peace that those who are given the gift of tongues come back with (27). While the post-coital implication is clear, it is also clear that a true outpouring of eulalia has yet to be given to Rachel (although Calla is the one who complains of God overlooking her).

When Rachel meets Nick Kazlik, she loses control of her voice, fumbles, titters, hesitates. By the time he kisses her, we have been pulled through such eulalic expectation that we are all longing for Nick Kazlik, his big bones, his searching hands. What Rachel envies Nick for is the freedom of his voice. (

> "Not so boxed-in. . . . More outspoken. More able to speak out." (88)

) Although earlier, Rachel is always rushing to "fill empty space with words" (62), when they are together, he does most of the talking; Rachel's voice is interiorized because she has finally come to a potentially eulalic connection. Just before making love to her, Nick comments, " 'that's the most talking you've done so far, Rachel' " (88). And yet, Rachel's pleading for touch has chorused the first half of the novel, the enpaged time it takes to get the reader to this sexual moment. Rachel's outcry at this crucial moment is internal (

> A brief searing hurt, and then his sex is in mine and I can feel him piercing warmly, unhurtfully. And—oh, Nick, I can't help this shuddering that is not desire, that's something I don't understand. I don't want to be this way. It's only my muscles, my skin, my nerves severed from myself, nothing to do with what I want to be. Forgive me. Forgive me. (91)

) and her begging for forgiveness is an address to the God/mortician/father/lover who are combined as the object of Rachel's desire. The lengthy withholding of sexual touch contributes to the novel's clamour up to this point and to a now truly eulalic speaking. From this moment on, Rachel speaks truthfully and feelingly. Eulalia has released her tongue as glossalalia did before.

The novel as an undertaking of physical expression cannot persist without an encounter with its own undertaker, especially because Rachel's cry is offered to the universal God/mortician/father/lover who constitutes the recipient of all our eulalic outbursts. Often, Rachel evokes "his voice," which we can deduce as that of her father, the mysterious mortician/king. (

> He is behind the door I cannot open. And his voice—his voice—so I know he is lying there among them, lying in state, king over them. He can't fool me. (19)

) He appears to be behind the door to Rachel's voice, and once she opens that eulalic door, she has to deal with undertakers and angelmakers. Sexual orgies are kin to funeral orgies; they belong together as an indictment of life's continuation. Rachel, unable to use the douche syringe to prevent potential life ("I'll never touch that contraption again." (117)), descends to that door she cannot open and knocks. Hector, who answers the door and becomes Rachel's guide through her dark night of the soul, lovers her in a different way. Rachel's knocking in the night is, of course, the insomnia of desire, and although she denies that to herself (

> He's wondering what I'm doing here, and now the notion occurs to me—maybe he thinks I've long admired him from afar and now at last have gone berserk enough to declare my burning spinster passion. I can hardly stop myself from laughing out loud. Hush, Rachel. Steady. (119)

) she does not stop herself from saying, " 'Let me come in,' " itself a sexual line. Hector takes her into the room marked "*Private*" (119), a kind of afterlife doctor's office, clean and sanitary; he then perches like a dwarf on the operating table and lays bare Rachel's voice. By talking about his business, he manages to give Rachel the confidence to reveal hers. (

> My voice has gone high and attenuated with some hurt I didn't know was there. The one long-tubed light burns with a harsh whiteness. Everything is the same as it was a moment ago, and yet the room looks all at once different, a room set nowhere, the stage-set of a drama that never was enacted. The steel is stainless, stained with the fingerprints of shadows, and behind a glass barrier the bottles and flasks bear legends which

> never could be read. I am sitting here, bound by my light wrists which touch the dark arms of this chair, bound as though by wires which may become live. And on the high altar squats a dwarf I've never seen before. (123-24)

) Hector as mortician/God/lover/father is underscored by his escorting Rachel on a tour of his re-modelled chapel. He leads Rachel "like a bride up the aisle" (125) and gives her the opportunity to worship at his particular shrine, to give way to another eulalic cry. (

> The blue light, and the chapel purged of all spirit, all spirits except the rye, and the sombre flashiness, and the terribly moving corniness of that hymn, and the hour, and the strangeness, and the plump well-meaning arm across my shoulders, and the changes in every place that go on without our knowing, and the fact that there is nothing here for me except what is here now— (127)

) When Rachel cries, Hector pats her shoulder and reassures her, but also says, " 'Listen . . . I don't know why I should say this, but you know what happens to me? At the crucial moment, my wife laughs. She says she can't help it—I look funny. Well, shit, I know she can't help it, but—' " (127-28). Hector's arm is around Rachel's shoulders; he describes to her his moment of orgasm, and its eulalic longing. They share that, Rachel and her mortician/lover, the dwarfed god of his own chapel and her father's replacement; and she sees him "living there behind his eyes" (128). That joint confession prepares us for Rachel's eulalic outcry to God, on her knees, (

> My God, I know how suspect You are. I know how suspect I am. (171)

) for her wish to apologize to the old men in the lobby of the Queen Victoria Hotel, apologize to them for not wanting to hear their longing (

> What I thought in those days was—whatever you feel, don't say or sing it, because if you do it will mortify me. If I went in there now, unbidden, young to them, strange in my white raincoat, and said *Forgive me*, they would think I had lost my mind. (162-63)

) So convention tries to ignore the eulalic needs of the body. Still, the body's cry persists; nothing can silence Rachel's wail of longing for love, for fulfillment, for children. From the moment Rachel enters a sexual conjunction with Nick until the end of the novel, her voice speaks its words of longing. And although it expresses longing and desire, that eulalic cry is its own fulfillment, and all of Rachel's disappointment, frustration, and misapprehension cannot silence it.

> Nothing is complicated. He inhabits whatever core of me there is. I can move outward to him, knowing he wants what I am, and I can receive him, whatever he is, whatever. And then this tender cruelty, always known to him but never before to me, the unmattering of what either of us is—only important that what we are doing should go on and go on and go on—
>
> "Nick—*Nick*—"
>
> Only his name. Only, at this moment, his name. The only word. (147-48)

This eulalic outcry is a name: lover/mortician/father/God gathered into one hearer, although Nick of course reminds Rachel, " 'I'm not God. I can't solve anything' " (148). All of Rachel's rending cry, including the imperative, "*Give me my children*" (148), is poured into this one, is concentrated here in Rachel's orgasmic eulalia. And even though, when Rachel calls Nick's mother and discovers that Nick has left, she answers his mother's question, " 'Who is speaking, please?' " (152), with silence, Rachel's crying out has now been unleashed and cannot stop. Despite all the subsequent reversals, her thwarted expectations and confusions of child and tumour, Rachel's tongue has been unloosed, and she can call the language of the future.

> *Make me to hear joy and gladness, that the bones which Thou hast broken may rejoice.* (201)

Rachel will. She has freed her speech, opened her mouth, cried out in that vocabulary that can never be glossed, that voice ululating its own longing. Rachel's cry echoes past its origin: her speaking offers the tongues of men and angels to all the heroines who have followed her eulalic story. Her bones have been opened, broken; they can now rejoice.

Works Consulted

Bowering, George. "That Fool of a Fear." *Margaret Laurence*. Ed. William New. Toronto: McGraw-Hill Ryerson Ltd., 1977. 161-76.

Daly, Mary. "The Calling of Spinsters: Spinning, not Swinging." *Gyn/Ecology*. Boston: Beacon Press, 1978. 392-94.

Djwa, Sandra. "False Gods and the True Covenant: Thematic Continuity Between Margaret Laurence and Sinclair Ross." *Margaret Laurence*. Ed. William New. Toronto: McGraw-Hill Ryerson Ltd., 1977. 66-84.

Forman, Denyse and Parameswaran, Uma. "Echoes and Refrains in the Canadian Novels of Margaret Laurence." *Margaret Laurence*. Ed. William New. Toronto: McGraw-Hill Ryerson Ltd., 1977. 85-100.

Harlow, Robert. "Lack of Distance." *Margaret Laurence*. Ed. William New. Toronto: McGraw-Hill Ryerson Ltd., 1977. 189-91.

Kroetsch, Robert. *What the Crow Said*. Toronto: General Publishing Ltd., 1978.

Laurence, Margaret. *A Jest of God*. 1966. Toronto: McClelland and Stewart, 1974.

_________. "Ten Years' Sentences." *Margaret Laurence*. Ed. William New. Toronto: McGraw-Hill Ryerson Ltd., 1977. 17-23.

Marlatt, Daphne. *Touch to My Tongue*. Edmonton: Longspoon Press, 1984.

Thomas, Clara. "The Novels of Margaret Laurence." *Margaret Laurence*. Ed. William New. Toronto: McGraw-Hill Ryerson Ltd., 1977. 55-65.

Helen M. Buss
University of Calgary

Margaret Laurence and the Autobiographical Impulse

IN HER AUTOBIOGRAPHICAL WORK, *Moments of Being*, Virginia Woolf tells of how her life and her art joined to create her novel *To The Lighthouse*:

> It is perfectly true that [my mother] obsessed me, in spite of the fact that she died when I was thirteen, until I was forty-four. Then one day walking round Tavistock Square I made up, as I sometimes make up my books, *To The Lighthouse*; in a great, apparently involuntary rush. One thing burst into another . . . my lips syllabling of their own accord as I walked. What blew the bubbles? Why then? I have no idea. But I wrote the book quickly; and when it was written, I ceased to be obsessed by my mother.
>
> I suppose that I did for myself what psycho-analysts do for their patients. I expressed some very long felt and deeply felt emotion. And in expressing it I explained it and then laid it to rest. (80)

Rarely does a writer reveal so plainly the autobiographical roots of her fictional work, the way in which one's identity as child of one's parent drives the currents of the imagination. It is that kind of impulse, that autobiographical impulse, to realize one's life, one's identity, by incorporating its characteristic patterns in creative endeavours that I wish to deal with in some of Margaret Laurence's works. Norman N. Holland compares this "identity theme" or patterning to the "mingling of sameness and difference as [in] a musical theme and variations" (Transactive 101). Holland asserts as well that "an 'identity theme' is determined by past events, yet paradoxically it is the only basis for future growth and, therefore, freedom" (Readers 61).

Freedom is the very word that Margaret Laurence used frequently in her public statements about the motivations and directions of her writing. She says that when she began writing the most important theme "seemed to be human freedom," and finds in later life "in a profound sense it still is human freedom." I think Laurence characteristically meant this in a political, societal sense, rather than in a personal, psychological sense, but she adds that "this [freedom] is linked with survival, which . . . has to be linked with some kind of growth and I would express this in terms of an inner freedom" (Thomas 67). In this second statement she is closer to agreeing with the therapeutic, identity-forming purposes of literature that Woolf marvels at. Although in an interview with Donald Cameron she says that if a novel is only a "therapeutic exercise" it should end up in the "bottom drawer" (Cameron 107), she regrets this judgement immediately and goes on to talk about how the "cultural pool" from which a writer comes shapes her. I would suggest that phrases like "cultural pool," "inner freedom" and references to "profound" freedom are euphemisms for an important motivation that lies behind all purposeful writing acts: the realization of one's identity theme.

I would like to explore three of Laurence's major works,

The Prophet's Camel Bell, A Bird in the House and *The Diviners*, in order to show how Laurence presents and realizes her selfhood in a set of symbolic structures that remain typical of her throughout her work, but which she is in the process of moderating and transforming in the interests of her "inner freedom." I choose these three works not only because they cover a large span of Laurence's writing career, but because the first is a directly autobiographical work in the form of a travel account, the second is indirectly autobiographical in that Laurence admits that all the short stories are based on her childhood family and life in Neepawa, and the third because it is a *künstlerroman* and thus is instructive in terms of Laurence's attitude to creativity, especially feminine creativity.

Throughout Margaret Laurence's work there appears a characteristic tendency to see the self divided into two contending elements, one a strongly authoritarian ego-self that she identifies consistently with male figures of authority, the other a wounded or damaged creative-self which she identifies with other male figures who often appear the victims of the first element. There is present, as well, from the very first work, another muted but growing force which I can only call Laurence's emerging consciousness of her female self. This growth factor eventually operates as an integrator which joins strength and creativity in—not a unity so much as a balance of elements—a kind of molecular binding of the atoms of a personality created by the artistic endeavour.

The Prophet's Camel Bell is part travelogue, part cultural exploration, part political commentary on Laurence's time spent in Somalia when it was still a British Protectorate. She went there because her husband Jack Laurence, an engineer, had been hired to create water "bellehs" to help the desert people during the dry seasons. Laurence signals the autobiographical nature of the work on its first page when she says: "in the excitement of the trip, the last thing in the world that would occur to you is that the strangest glimpses you may have of any creature in the distant lands will be those you catch of yourself" (1). The "you" of her introduction quickly becomes the very autobiographical "I" of the young idealistic, politically leftist Canadian girl, "unburdened with Knowledge" (1), as Laurence puts it, who runs smash into a culture so foreign that it causes her to question her most deeply held convictions about herself and the nature of the world.

In this questioning process, Laurence, in a way that is typical of women autobiographers, uses her relationships with others to show her personal psychic journey. Three Somalian men offer her an understanding of their culture which aids in her self-discovery. Her first mentor is Hersi, the "teller of tales," who begins her education in Somalian poetry. Her artist-self makes a strong identification with this man who is not only a story-teller like herself, but an outsider, as she is in his country, for he has lost his tribal place and finds no new place in the white "realm of clerks and book-keepers" (160). Just as she has found that her position as woman in a Moslem world disadvantages her as inquiring reporter/writer, so Hersi is disadvantaged as an oral poet by his speech impediment. Although Laurence has great admiration for Hersi's dramatic ability, "for he was an artist and he gave to each performance the very best of which he was capable" (160), she laments his lonely position in life:

> Hersi was caught, partly by the past, the memories and handed down sagas of Haji Musa Farah's achievements, and partly by his own frail present-day. Only through jobs with the Ingrese [the English] could he utilize what accomplishments he had, those of reading and writing. Yet this education was so limited that his position could never be really secure. Nor was his education sufficient to enable him ever to break away from his tribe. He needed an established status in both worlds, but he achieved it in neither. (157)

Such a view of the artist, as exile held by traditions that inhibit and haunt him, his talents unrecognized or undeveloped, his creativity damaged by physical and psychic wounds, is to become a familiar one in Laurence's work.

Laurence's need to help such characters out of their predicaments is indicated by her confession of her unwise meddling in their personal lives, in which she discovers that she does more harm than good. Her close identification with such underdogs is most aptly indicated by her attempts to teach her cook, Mohamed, how to read and write. Her failure in this regard she attributes to her overconfidence in her ability to change things through direct but limited action: "we both under-estimated the difficulties. But it was I who should have known better, simply because I was literate and ought to have had some comprehension of the fact that literacy is not acquired magically in a few days." The young Laurence asks herself: "What else had I under-estimated?" (165). It would seem that she has underestimated the complex nature of the human personality, and the difficulty of personal growth, as again and again she fails to solve the problems of those Somalis with whom she most closely identifies.

A Somali man with whom she does not wish to identify any part of herself also causes problems for Laurence. An old warrior, Abdi, is hired as a driver for Laurence and her husband in their journeys through the desert in search of belleh sites. The old man is "taciturn and uncommunicative. . . . he was extremely proud" but expresses a "servility" towards the couple "that bothered us" (179). Eventually, after the old warrior has been responsible for saving their lives, the Laurences find that he becomes so authoritarian and abusive to other employees that they have to, with much regret, fire him. This leads Laurence to investigate more closely how she and her husband are perceived by their Somalian employees and finds to her horror that they perceive the young liberal-thinking couple from Canada as exactly the same type as the other "Ingrese," the all-powerful and hated imperialists from which the Laurences have been at pains to separate themselves. Laurence is confused and disturbed by the Abdi affair, especially since she felt a "bond" of friendship with the old man, despite his behaviour, and only much later in her life, when reading Mannoni's *The Psychology of Colonization*, does she realize her own implication in the authoritarian, imperialistic system that created the hatred between colonizer and colonized. She describes her feeling as "the shock of recognition one sometimes feels when another's words have a specific significance in terms of one's own experiences" (188)

The recognition of her own involvement in an authoritarian world is only on the political level at this point in her life. She has not yet begun to recognize that in Abdi, she was seeing a part of her self. That recognition must wait until Laurence begins to write of her own people.

At the same time as Laurence begins to be fascinated by these two opposite types of male personalities, there appears in her work a muted but gradually resonating concern with the feminine. However, this concern does not at first emerge through close and affectionate identification with personalities that represent the feminine, but rather by a series of situations observed by a wary and distant Laurence, who seems most intent on avoiding any connection with the disadvantages of being female. In Somalian society she sees what it means to be female in its most distressing forms. Some Somalian women hear that Laurence is administering first aid and distributing pain killers to the men in camp and come to ask her to give them some relief from the pain they experience during menstruation and sexual intercourse. This pain is caused by the ritual surgeries performed on them at puberty. She realizes their complaint is beyond her medical expertise and asks: "What should I do? give them a couple of five-grain aspirin? Even if they had money to buy future pills, which they had not, the lunatic audacity of shoving a mild pill at their total situation was more than I could stomach." She describes their reaction and in doing so aptly describes the "total situation" of women in patriarchal society: "They nodded their heads, unprotestingly. They had not really believed I would give them anything. Women had always lived with pain. Why should it ever be any different? They felt they ought not to have asked. They hid their faces in their cloths for a moment, then spoke of other things" (64).

In a similar way Laurence becomes aware of the ways in which women perpetuate the exploitation of their own sex. A "jes" or "tea-shop-cum-brothel" takes up residence near their camp and Laurence discovers that an eight-year-old girl, young Asha, is a child prostitute. The little girl comes to Laurence in her free moments to have her hair combed. Laurence wants to help, but realizes that Asha's fate is controlled by an old "crone" who runs the jes and who will not easily relinquish her means of livelihood. Since she does not have the power to change Asha's life completely and any partial interference might just make it worse, Laurence decides to do nothing. However, the situation, like others involving women, haunts her. She concludes: "Asha's half-wild half-timid face with its ancient eyes will remain with me always, a reproach and a question" (142). The archetypal nature of the description and the use of the future tense emphasize the importance of this incident to Laurence's own sense of self. The question that "will remain with me always" becomes for Laurence, in her Canadian works, an enquiry into the imprisonment of the female in patriarchal society and the strategies with which individual women cope with that imprisonment. This last will be closely related to her discoveries regarding the nature of female creativity.

Throughout *The Prophet's Camel Bell*, Laurence continually remarks on the strange ways in which women seek to empower themselves despite their situation. All the while she maintains her own position as a sort of honorary man, identifying with and participating in her husband's activities. Not unexpectedly, it is the central fact of femininity, pregnancy, that prevents Laurence from continuing in this status. As a pregnant woman confined to town she is forced to begin to notice the much despised "memsahibs," the wives of British officials, whom previously she has scorned as the ultimate parasites of the imperialistic world. She finds that even here there are exceptions.

She meets one woman who has worked at distributing rations in the desert during the worst of a famine, an act that Laurence understands because she has lived outside the towns. She observes: "to portion out the careful rations to their clamouring desperation—this took courage. Such courage I knew I did not possess" (223). And later when her own translation of Somalian poetry is well underway, she meets an English woman with a similar interest in African poetry and folk-tales. But with the discovery of the first female with whom she can enthusiastically identify, Laurence finds a typical limitation:

> I was about to suggest that she drop over to my bungalow the following day for a beer and a continuation of the discussion. I recalled in time, however, that this was not possible. One does not ask the Governor's wife to drop over for a beer. This kind of formality, which prevents people from talking with one another, seemed idiotic to me then, and it still does. (234)

The idea that female solidarity is limited because of women's relationships to men becomes a prominent issue in the stories of *A Bird in the House*.

But more than an issue of sexual politics, the subject has importance as it reveals Laurence's preoccupations with identity. The moment she wants to have a beer with the Governor's wife is the first time in *Prophet* where Laurence's fascination with another fixes on a woman. The fact that her enthusiasm is immediately prevented by a propriety of the patriarchal world is indicative of how male-defined the personality of the young Laurence is. After all, this is the young woman who has broken all the rules of the life of a "memsahib" in Somalia. Why not this small regulation? But this is a book about the development of quite a young person (Laurence was 25 at the time of her Somalian experiences), and the account is centred on the young intellectual woman's male identification. It is not until the stories of *A Bird in the House* that we see a gradual shift taking place, as Laurence, still on the surface preoccupied with the two types of male personalities I have outlined, becomes aware of a strong feminine world, existing seemingly only to support and nurture its patriarchal masters, but engaged in a continual, though perhaps largely unconscious, subversion of that world. It is the discovery of this dichotomy through the writing of the *Bird* stories that leads Laurence to a more fully mature identity theme.

* * *

The stories of *A Bird in the House* are, as Laurence has said, "directly drawn from my own childhood" (Cameron 106), but they are autobiographical in a more important way than in their real-life characters and situations. Laurence says that she thinks "all writing . . . is a kind of self-discovery. In a profound sense there is something of you in all your characters; they are almost all of them in a way disguises for you, in one or other of your aspects, and very often you discover things about yourself through the characters that you hadn't known before" (Cameron 100). Laurence confesses that through the writing of *The Stone Angel* and the *Bird* collection she found that there was "a good deal of the matriarch in me. I have to watch this very closely with my own kids and always have" (Cameron 99). It is interesting that Laurence connects her urge to be a "matriarch" with the characteristics of stubbornness and authoritarianism which are the principal ingredients of the grandfather figure in the short stories. This stems from an insufficient understanding of matriarchal characteristics, and in this collection, although Laurence is beginning to recognize female strength, she has not yet begun to get over the fear such strength causes in those of us, men and women, raised inside the patriarchy.

On the surface, *A Bird in the House* is preoccupied with the character of Timothy Connor and his effect on the lives of others. He, like the old warrior Abdi in *Prophet*, is used to being in charge. But unlike Abdi, Grandfather Connor has not yet been challenged by any great societal change, so the men and women who surround him still serve his ego in angry silence. As well as authority figures, Laurence is fascinated by figures of male creativity, who in this book are directly harmed by Grandfather Connor. Most prominent among these is Chris, the central character of "Horses of the Night." Even his name indicates his Christlike passivity. Chris has learned, as Vanessa puts it, to "simply . . . be absent, elsewhere" in a psychological sense, when attacked (133). This ability to separate his emotions from himself allows Chris to live three years in Timothy's household. Later, when the only chance to escape his narrow rural life is offered by going to war, he writes to Vanessa that "they" could make his "body march and even kill," but he had "fooled them. He didn't live inside it any more." Vanessa realizes that the cause of Chris's eventual madness and confinement in a mental asylum is "only the heartbreaking extension of that way he'd always had of distancing himself from the absolute unbearability of battle" (153).

These short stories verify what *Prophet* only suggests, that Laurence sees the patriarchal world as divided into victor and victim, as even seemingly decent men like Vanessa's father suffer a lifetime from the wounds inflicted by the unfairness of patriarchal demands. At the end of the collection Vanessa realizes that her grandfather needs no monument because he "proclaimed himself in my veins" (206), just as Laurence admits that "when I got to the end of those stories, I realized . . . I was an awful lot like him" (Cameron 99). The grandfather figure may represent the full realization of a powerful force in the writer's personality; one that makes her insist on the strength of her own beliefs, her own ways, but which, as her fascination with the figures of damaged creativity demonstrate, conflicts with her more creative aspects.

In *A Bird in the House* the element that is to eventually allow the integration of these two opposing factors is a constant undercurrent. Laurence gives more and more attention to female figures, principally in revealing the strategies they take in dealing with the powerful patriarchal world in which they live. Vanessa's grandmothers offer contrasting adaptations. Timothy's wife has developed a reputation for saintliness which is rewarded by the respect of those around her. Yet when she dies and her children speak in awe of her "angel" qualities, her son Terrence observes: "Can you feature going to bed with an angel. . . . It doesn't bear thinking about." To his sister's angry attempt to silence any criticism of their saintly mother Terrence replies: "All this angel business gets us into really deep water" (86). The suggestion is that female saintliness may be part of the problem of patriarchy, not part of the solution. When Vanessa observes the results of choosing to be a queen in the patriarchal world rather than a saint, as her Grandmother MacLeod has done, she discovers that her petite and queenly grandmother, although undisputed ruler in her home, has no power outside it. When her last son is dead Vanessa sees that in her grandmother's world, "a family whose men are gone is no family at all" (111). Grandmother MacLeod is shipped off to Winnipeg to live with a married daughter, her power fading around her like a mirage.

When Vanessa looks around at the next generation of women, her mother's generation, she sees only her Aunt Edna, fighting her economic and emotional imprisonment in her father's house with a subversive but largely ineffective humour, and her own mother, who at times seems in training for saintliness like Grandmother Connor before her.

The only figure of strength that Vanessa finds is the strange and almost absurd figure of Noreen, the hired girl, who enters briefly into Vanessa's life in the story that gives the collection its name. Noreen gains interest because she has kept her powerful imagination alive through her religious beliefs, and because she exudes an aura of physical confidence unfamiliar to Vanessa in the other women she knows. Vanessa says that "I began to think of her as a sorceress, someone not quite of this earth" (100). When Noreen's prediction that a bird in the house means a death in the house comes true with Vanessa's father's death, the young girl instinctively blames the most powerful female figure she knows, the woman whose prediction came true. I find it telling that Vanessa should have this instinctive reaction, since traditionally in the archetypal images of woman that come to us through patriarchal interpretation, woman is seen not only as the giver of life but the taker of life. The words that Laurence gives Vanessa to describe her anger at Noreen are also telling: "I hit Noreen as hard as I could. . . . as though she were a prison all around me and I was battling to get out" (109). Indeed, in this book "womanhood" does imprison all the female figures, a womanhood that must be either weak but approved or strong but unacceptable. Even the juvenile writings of young Vanessa, in which she portrays a "barbaric queen, beautiful and terrible" (64), are stymied when she realizes the completeness of the imprisonment of the women she knows in real life. Noreen is an important figure for another reason. Although I do not think that Laurence is recommending Noreen's preoccupation with Ouija boards and fundamentalist religion as a healthy expression of female strength, I do think she is implying that to be strong as well as good, the feminine must in some way be connected with the divine.

The only positive realization of female strength in this collection comes in its last pages when Beth, Vanessa's mother, tells her that she has actively sought support, even from Vanessa's grandfather, in order to send the young girl to college. Beth confesses how the feared patriarch once prevented her from a similar ambition because he "didn't believe in education for women then" (203). With her mother's new show of support Vanessa realizes "the tigress" her mother hides "beneath her exterior" (202).

Interestingly, Laurence has the older Vanessa, narrator of the stories, confess that "of all the deaths in the family, it was hers [her mother's] that remained unhealed the longest" (206). This "unhealed" quality is very close to the feeling the young Laurence has about the child prostitute Asha, in *Prophet*, whose eyes "remain with me always, a reproach and a question." I think that at the end of the short story collection, Laurence has realized the part of herself represented by the figure of the old warrior in *Prophet* and by the grandfather figure, and she has brought more fully to consciousness the qualities represented by characters such as Hersi the storyteller and Chris. The third element, shown by the growing number of female personages in her work, particularly imprisoned females, is the factor that will be much more the writer's preoccupation in *The Diviners*.

* * *

I must admit to some hesitation in bringing the idea of the theme of the writer's identity to the interpretation of *The Diviners*. Philippe Lejeune points out in "Autobiography in the Third Person" that a writer may offer three different kinds of contracts with the reader: "fiction, the reading of which does not depend upon what the reader knows about the author, or autobiographical fiction which lends itself to an ambiguous reading, or autobiography, in which referential reading and author's posture are combined" (Lejeune 28). The last two types are represented by *A Bird in the House* and *Prophet*, but since in all fairness *The Diviners* must be considered of the first type, not dependent on knowledge of the writer, how do I rationalize breaking my "contract" with its writer? I do so on several grounds. First of all because it is a *künstlerroman* and as such inevitably invites comparison of the writer's life and the artist's life as portrayed in the fiction; secondly, because in concentrating on the "differences and sameness" repetitions of an "identity theme," rather than simple comparison of biographical detail, I hope to avoid the reductiveness of biographical fallacy; and finally because Laurence has, indirectly, indicated how close the consciousness of Morag is to her own. She described to Donald Cameron the feeling she had after writing to a friend, that the character she was writing about (which at the time of the interview would have been Morag) had written the letter, not herself: "I didn't write that letter, *she* did. It was written in *her* idiom, *her* character, and it scared the hell out of me. I thought, Who am I? Every novelist has this terrible feeling from time to time: Who am I? because you feel almost that you may exist only in your characters and not have a character of your own" (Cameron 102). The feeling of being possessed by one's characters works both ways: the writer could not produce a persona as deeply felt and fully realized as Morag unless such a consciousness were in large part her own, one struggling to enter fully into the world.

But before exploring the ways in which Laurence uses Morag to enhance the feminine in her identity theme, we should look at the ways in which the two opposing male elements come to maturity in her last novel. Here we find the fullest expression of her identification with male figures who represent damaged creativity. In Jules and Christie we find the culmination of Hersi and Chris and all the other maimed and tortured sensitive men of other Laurence works. And it becomes quite clear which qualities they possess that Laurence is in the process of incorporating into her own identity. Just as Hersi was admired for his dramatic ability as a story-teller, and Chris for his inventive and independent mind, Christie powerfully maintains his beliefs and traditions against all opposition and insists on the legitimacy of his own language. Christie's tales of Piper Gunn are the ground on which Morag builds her "scribbler" full of stories of Piper Gunn's woman, and thus begins her life as a writer. More importantly, by giving her a love of language, particularly oral language, Christie profoundly affects Morag's life. For example, when Morag finally works up the nerve to cut her ties with Brooke Skelton it is Christie's language she uses to do it. After finally telling Brooke the "everlasting Christly truth" about their unhealthy relationship, she realizes she has spoken in Christie's words and thinks: "I do not know the sound of my own voice. Not yet, anyhow" (256-57). And from this point on the young writer, Morag, goes on most deliberately to find her "own voice" in both her life and her work.

For Laurence the importance of the figure of Christie and of finding one's own "voice" is indicated by the orality of the language of this book. *The Diviners* is dramatic tale-telling at its best. Not just the embedded stories of Jules and Christie, but Morag's own voice and the stories she tells in that voice, contain the intimacy and dramatic qualities of a voice telling a story aloud. In fact, there are times when Laurence cannot resist the urge to tell her fiction in play format as illustrated by Morag's conversations with Catherine Parr Traill.

Although, in many ways, Christie represents in his character and his language the ways in which the creative female writer incorporates that part of the patriarchy which has been excluded and demeaned, it is in Jules that we see how the female writer's need for a libidinal but unrepressive connection with masculinity is achieved. I have explored this phenomenon of the male "muse" in my essay on Laurence's "dark lovers," and so will only summarize the characteristics of this figure, who in a very real sense becomes the lively animus of the Morag character in *The Diviners* (Dark Lovers 97-107). He is, in all Laurence's Manawaka novels, dark skinned, dark haired, native Canadian or native in appearance, sexually provocative, and most importantly "forbidden" to the protagonist because in some way he is the despised outsider in respectable society. Jules is the culmination and most complete expression of several characters in other works, and is vital to the liberation of Morag's artistic self. This happens most obviously on the sexual level when Jules thinks that he is her "shaman" releasing her from Brooke's domination. "You were doing magic, to get away," he tells Morag after they make love. And that magic is certainly part of the role Jules plays in her life. But more importantly, it is the long-term result of that love-making that changes Morag. As she says to Jules: "I know that whatever I'm going to do next, or wherever I go, it'll have to be on my own" (270). What Morag does next is live on her own as a self-supporting writer and single parent, giving birth to Pique who becomes the female figure who provides the motivation for Morag's opus, the story she is telling in *The Diviners*.

At the same time as Laurence's writer-figure is quite literally incorporating into her identity the abused but creative male victim of the patriarchy, she is making her peace with the victimizer. In the character of Brooke Skelton we see the figure of the proud and intolerant warrior Abdi and the dominant and feared patriarch Timothy Connor brought into the contemporary world. In our world, where patriarchy still holds sway, but often in disguised forms, phenomena like Brooke Skelton become typical of its disguises. As the well-mannered and pleasant professor of English Literature, he would seem to be far from the other authority figures in Laurence's work. But he prevents the progress of the feminine as surely as Timothy Connor prevents his daughter from going to college. Brooke not only becomes the authority on Morag's life-style, clothing, intellectual development and writing production, but through her deeply felt need to "belong," in a sexual/psychological sense, he controls her femininity. Not only does he refuse to let her conceive, but even asks her "have you been a good girl, love?" (245) before allowing her the "gift" of his entry into her.

In *A Bird in the House*, Laurence lets Vanessa turn away from Grandfather Connor's tears and therefore from the possibility of the humanity beneath his authoritarian surface. In *The Diviners*, she allows Morag to glimpse the cause of Brooke's need to control those around him. When she discovers that as a child, Brooke was disciplined by his father by being displayed publicly with a sign around his neck reading "I Am Bad," she tries to sympathize with him as an equal, but Brooke side-steps what might make their relationship more open, more growth oriented, by saying "At least it taught me to stand up for myself" (219). Standing up for himself for Brooke means becoming a military school sergeant at age eight. He internalizes the patriarchal imperative of victim or victor and never gets "pushed around" (218) by anyone. Such a man can only build a marriage in which he controls, and although Morag must leave such a situation in the interests of her own freedom, Laurence allows her to understand its roots before she does so. She also allows her a measure of forgiveness, as Morag expresses a silent wish years later after seeing Brooke with his second wife: "May we forgive one another for what neither of us could help" (336).

Recognition, acceptance and forgiveness are only a portion of the growth in identity shown in *The Diviners*. Most importantly, the character of Morag allows a partial realization of feminine identity. In my study of mother and daughter relationships in Laurence's work (*Mother and Daughter* 64-76) I emphasized Morag's special place in the Laurence canon by quoting from *The Symbolic Quest* by E. Whitmont. The passage bears repeating here to illuminate Morag's importance to Laurence's identity theme:

> One might speculate on the possibility that there may be no archetypal pattern available in western Christian culture—that is to say no archetypal pattern that has been accepted by this culture—that would enable certain types of women to find their true individuality in terms of their femininity. The basic rejection and denigration of feminine values as compared to masculine values is the heritage of our historically patriarchal

> culture. This has resulted in a situation in which the feminine individuation problem has become a pioneering task that is perhaps meant to usher in a new period of culture. (Whitmont 214)

Margaret Laurence plays a part in that "pioneering" effort to find satisfactory patterns by which women may find their "true individuality." In creating Morag she creates for herself and others, not an heroic ideal to be strived for, not a role model to be emulated, but rather an identity process. Morag is not really a character in the traditional sense, but a feminine mode of questing, one which involves the articulation through language of the mutable self as it forms and reforms through a lifetime, creating the prismatic reality of the creative woman.

I would suggest here only some of the surfaces of such a prism. The journey of the creative woman is very much like Psyche's in the tale of Eros and Psyche, in which we see a representative of the feminine refusing to accept her position in the darkness imposed by her god/lover. She seeks light/knowledge and in doing so sets off on a hard road of consciousness which leads her eventually to accomplish the tasks assigned by the Goddess and receive the reward of her Eros and her girl child (Neumann 3-56). In the same way Morag comes into the possession of her own "eros," her own libidinal self, because she will not accept the male-definitions offered her, and chooses instead a way of life that demands constant self-examination and continual revision of her directions, her ethics and her expression of herself. This way of life involves not a rejection of the patriarchal past, but rather its embodiment in the female self. Such embodiment is expressed in *The Diviners* through Morag's incorporation of the tales of Jules and Christie in her own story, the position of understanding and forgiveness she achieves vis-a-vis Brooke Skelton, and the sense of creativity renewed and extended in the figure of Pique.

But the greatest indication of the writer's sense of the feminine can be seen in the female characters that fill the pages of *The Diviners*. Together they offer an epic view of all the ways in which women are imprisoned and imprison themselves and the ways in which they are struggling for that very "inner freedom" that was so important to Laurence. There are the Gerson sisters and their mother, building their positive matriarchy in humour and love; the absurd but delightful Fan Brady re-visioning the Eve figure with her pet snake. There are the women who appear to have accepted their places in the patriarchy but nevertheless facilitate another's freedom. Prin, Morag's stepmother, names her "mooner" and thus begins Morag's mythologization of her own identity as "a mooner." "That sounds nice," thinks the young Morag. "It means somebody who moons around, dawdling and thinking. But to her it means something else. Some creature from another place, 'another planet' " (51). As well, there is Eva Winkler, the ultimate victim, but through whom, ironically, Morag realizes her fierce ability to protect, and who finally is able, in a strange sense, to give a Manawakan acceptance to Morag's illegitimate offspring when she meets Pique in the town graveyard and does not turn away from her.

And most importantly, there is Pique herself, through whose birth Morag realizes the fullness of her creative self. Interestingly, the Psyche myth, of which *The Diviners* seems so often reflective, does not tell us about the journey of Psyche through to the raising of her daughter. Laurence's book does, and this is what places it in that "pioneering" category of artistic endeavours that Whitmont writes of in *The Symbolic Quest*. The relationship of Pique and her mother Morag underlies every moment of Morag's narrative. There would be no narrative if "something about Pique's going, apart from the actual departure itself, was unresolved in Morag's mind" (5). With this need to resolve the memories begin. Throughout the book it is Pique's arrivals and departures, her questions and her accusations, her youthful successes and failures, that stimulate the autobiographical project in the mother. This recreation of self in language by Morag is echoed at all times in Pique's songs, and reaches its fulfillment when Morag gives Pique her maternal blessing, the blessing of a mother who has realized the divine in herself when she tells her daughter to "Go with God" (450).

In her essay "Writing Womanly: theory and practice," Carolyn Hlus summarizes what many Canadian writing women have said about maternality and creativity. Hlus enunciates this trinity: "My Mother. My daughter. My/Self. Every woman extending backwards into her mother and forever forward into her daughter" (291). Or as Virginia Woolf put it in *A Room of One's Own*: "We think back through our mothers if we are women" (114). Or as Morag puts it just after her final parting from Pique: "Look ahead into the past, and back into the future, until the silence" (453). And with this she finishes her telling.

It is my conviction that Laurence came to only a partial realization of the feminine in her identity theme in writing the fiction of Morag and her daughter Pique. There are dimensions of maternality which that book cannot explore because of the limits of its fictional construct. Principally, these limits involve the situation of Morag's orphanhood, and that she has no surviving family members through which she can explore the lives of her parents, particularly her mother, to find herself. I would predict that subject matter will be central to the unpublished memoirs that Laurence completed before her death. When Laurence's last autobiographical enterprise is in the hands of readers, it will become clearer whether she realizes the fullness of her search for the feminine through her exploration of those vital female ancestors: her mother who died when she was very young and her maternal aunt who raised her. Until I have read her last book I refrain from making my fullest conclusions on the realization of the autobiographical impulse in the work of Margaret Laurence.

I would, however, like to conclude with Laurence's own assessment of the development of the "themes" of her writing. Although the political language in which it is framed does not allow for the kind of "confession" that Virginia Woolf made in *Moments of Being*, it does have a personal reference similar to that which I have been proposing:

> My sense of social awareness, my feelings of anti-colonialism, anti-authoritarianism, had begun, probably, in embryo form in my own childhood; they had been nurtured during my college years and immediately afterwards, in the North Winnipeg of the old Left; they had developed considerably through my African experience. It was not very difficult to relate this experience to my own land, which had been under the sway of Britain once and was now under the colonial sway of America. But these developing feelings also related very importantly to my growing awareness of the dilemma and powerlessness of women, the tendency of women to accept male definitions of ourselves, to be self-deprecating and uncertain, and to rage inwardly. The quest for physical and spiritual freedom, the quest for relationships of equality and communication—these themes run through my fiction and are connected with the theme of survival, not mere physical survival, but a survival of the spirit, with human dignity and the ability to give and receive love. (Ivory 24)

Works Consulted

Buss, Helen M. "Margaret Laurence's Dark Lovers: Sexual Metaphor and the Movement Toward Individuation, Hierogamy and Mythic Narrative in Four Manawaka Books." *Atlantis* II. 2 (Spring 1986): 97-107.

__________. *Mother and Daughter Relationships in the Manawaka Works of Margaret Laurence*. English Literature Series #34.

Victoria: Victoria U.P., 1985.

Cameron, Donald. "Margaret Laurence: The Black Celt Speaks of Freedom." *Conversations with Canadian Novelists*. Toronto: Macmillan, 1973. 96-115.

Hlus, Carolyn. "Writing Womanly: Theory and Practice." *A Mazing Space, Writing Canadian Women Writing*. Ed. S. Neuman and S. Kamboureli. Edmonton: Longspoon/NeWest, 1986. 287-97.

Holland, Norman N. *5 readers reading*. New Haven and London: Yale U.P., 1975.

__________. "A Transactive Account of Transactive Criticism." *Poetics* 7 (1978): 177-89.

Laurence, Margaret. *A Bird in the House*. 1963. Toronto: McClelland and Stewart, 1974.

__________. *The Diviners*. 1974. Toronto: McClelland and Stewart, 1978.

__________. "Ivory Tower or Grass Roots? The Novelist as Socio-Political Being." *A Political Art: Essays and Images in Honour of George Woodcock*. Ed. William New. Vancouver: University of British Columbia Press, 1978. 15-25.

__________. *The Prophet's Camel Bell*. 1963. Toronto: McClelland and Stewart, 1965.

Lejeune, Philippe. "Autobiography in the Third Person." *New Literary History* 9. 1 (Autumn 1977): 27-50.

Maron, Mary. "The Other Voice: Autobiographies of Women Writers." *Autobiography: Essays Theoretical and Critical*. Ed. James Olney. Princeton: Princeton U.P., 1980. 207-35.

Neumann, Eric. *Amor and Psyche: The Psychic Development of the Feminine*. Trans. Ralph Manheim. New York: Pantheon Books, 1956.

Thomas, Clara. "A Conversation about Literature: An Interview with Margaret Laurence and Irving Layton." *Journal of Canadian Fiction* I. I (Winter 1972): 65-69.

Whitmont, E. *The Symbolic Quest*. New York: Putnam, 1969.

Woolf, Virginia. *Moments of Being*. Ed. Jeanne Schulkind. New York and London: Harcourt, Brace, Jovanovich, 1976.

__________. *A Room of One's Own*. 1929. London: Hogarth Press, 1954.

Herbert Zirker
University of Trier

Metaphoric Mapping in Margaret Laurence's Narrative

> Now when I was a little chap I had a passion for maps. I would . . . lose myself in all the glories of exploration.
>
> —Marlow in *Heart of Darkness*

IN THIS PAPER I should like to take as my point of departure the concept of "mapping" elaborated on and applied to Canadian contexts by Aritha van Herk in her article "Mapping as Metaphor," published in 1982. Her initial observations with a view to the, shall I say, down-to-earth suitability of the term are as follows:

> It is no wonder that the concept of mapping is so inherent to the way we see ourselves—as nation, as people, as literature. Because we are such a new country, we have almost perfect records of our own charting and because of our youth, we continue to participate in that mapping; it remains both an on-going process and a metaphor for our particularity. (75)

Mapping is a figurative term, a synonym for planning things, organizing, coordinating programs or identifying a state of affairs—"mapping it out in a mental sense" (Cooley 23). What I would like to underscore, however, is the practical and scientific use of the term *mapping*, which is not really lost even in its figurative, metaphoric use. It has rather regained, reassumed currency in its function of denoting geographic, cartographic and technical skills.

Aritha van Herk has drawn our attention to the speed with which the seemingly neutral business of the surveyors' and the land developers' map-making becomes a negative thing, "the foul business" of "creating borders," of "fixing limits" instead of opening up "the range of freedom" (76). *Mapping* in its negative aspect has lent itself to politico-moralistic invective, and I find the ambivalence towards such enterprising exploits as the geographer's and explorer's trade appropriate, as it is expressed in one of Voltaire's polemical asides in his *Histoire de l'empire de Russie sous Pierre le Grand*:

> La géographie est encore de tous les arts celui qui a la plus besoin de être perfectionné, et l'ambition a jusqu'ici pris plus de soin de dévaster la terre que de la décrire. (466)

We can hardly escape the semantic ambiguity of the term *mapping*, with its descriptive, denotative and denunciative aspects: "The explorers and colonists did not passively record; they imposed their map on place regardless of whether or not the grid they chose was always appropriate" (77). And equating fiction writers with cartographers, Aritha van Herk points out that "the novelist insinuates, pervades, invades" (77), thus using the vocabulary of the invader/explorer and developer while at the same time invoking the semantics of creativity, either literary or critical, or else of the creativity of understanding, orienting, interpreting—exploring new areas, "territories" of the real, of the mind.

Literature and criticism themselves become suspect when

terms of science and technology are used this way in their service. When we look at the above uses of *exploration*, i.e. as a term of literary criticism, the deliberate and reiterated *rapprochement* to the prospector's and cartographer's "useful" activities, there seems to be an inherent desire to give literature and criticism similarly utilitarian characteristics. As if the job of creating and interpreting texts were in need of the sort of justification which would render such dubious activities more palatable to the utilitarian-minded "common man."

I am indeed reminded of an early instance of this: Louise M. Rosenblatt's book *Literature as Exploration*, first published in 1938. In the preface she states: "My aim is to demonstrate that the study of literature can have a very real and even central relation to the points of growth in the social and cultural life of a democracy" (vii). We notice an apologetic undercurrent, very likely *vis-à-vis* the imperial, even imperialistic claims of the supposedly more exact social sciences. There is a hankering for an all-embracing method and mode of explication in literature with the question of "relevance" looming on the critical horizon. The same apologetic overtones, if slightly more sure of themselves, can be felt in this:

> The title of this book should be understood as a metaphor, not a limiting definition. The word *exploration* is designed to suggest primarily that the experience of literature, far from being for the reader a passive process of absorption is the form of intense personal activity. . . . (Rosenblatt vii)

And part of her task is "to sketch some of the personal and social benefits that may flow from such literary discovery" (viii).

Nowadays, when several schools of reader-response research are firmly institutionalized in the academic establishment and are flourishing no less than New Criticism in its heyday—when we have come to speak of "writerly" and "readerly" approaches, L.M. Rosenblatt's apologetic observations of decades ago may appear tame. Indeed, they were then still largely concerned with claiming the potential of an educational practice operative in the talk of exploration. Nevertheless it seems feasible to be reminded of some of the origins of our methods of interpretation and their naming. It appears that as long as we can put the geographers' and the cartographers' explorative tools safely into Pooh Bear's "Useful Pot" of common respectability, the elusive job of creating and interpreting "mere" texts will become more solid. The dreaming of literature will receive some sanctification from the exact disciplines of the Other Culture and thus become more digestible.

In borrowing from Aritha van Herk's comments I am not concerned merely with bringing out these apologetic aspects of the uses of the language of science in literary criticism. What needs to be emphasized is that by using the map as critical metaphor we have a real and concrete object at hand. The familiar set of instruments this gives us reinforces the real-estate value of the image, even when transposed to the "unreal estate" (Nabokov 40) realms of narrative structures. These instruments draw upon and are drawn into "the world man constructs" where "anything goes that can be imagined" (Frye 8).

A perfect object of this description, both as a thing in nature and an image in fiction, is the loon in Margaret Laurence's story "The Loons" (*BH* 96-108). If Laurence was right when she said "A title should, if possible, be like a line of poetry—capable of saying a great deal with hardly any words" (*HS* 203), then this is a case in point. The loon is an image that is often treated as a cliché. A recent instance occurs in a review of *The Apprentice's Tale* by Hugh Mackay Ross, where Peter C. Newman admires "the cadence of seasons passing" that Ross catches in his reminiscences, or "hearing a loon's lonely lullaby." Newman quotes Ross:

> a long, *melancholy* wail, bursting suddenly into a *shriek of maniacal laughter*. Even today, when I hear it, I get shivers up my spine, for it brings back almost forgotten memories. The cry of the loon, to me, is the call of Canada. (Newman 55, italics mine).

The *locus classicus*, of which these touching lines of regional-patriotic lore are a close enough echo, occurs in Laurence's story in a key passage:

> No one can ever describe that ululating sound, the crying of loons, and no one who has heard it, can ever forget it. Plaintive, and yet with a quality of chilling mockery, those voices belonged to a world separated by aeons from our neat world of summer cottages and the lighted lamps of home. (*BH* 102)

Of course we know that this passage and the loons in it pursue aims and work in ways qualitatively different from what is expressed in the earlier quotation. Let me therefore refer to some of the plot elements and characters of the story very briefly.

Vanessa, the narrator, has been endowed with some of Laurence's autobiographical experience and family context. Piquette, who is Vanessa's classmate from the Métis Tonnerre family, the daughter of Lazarus Tonnerre of a group of outcasts who live in squalid circumstances at the edge of town, is invited by Vanessa's father, Dr. MacLeod, to spend the summer with them at their lake cottage. Piquette suffers from tuberculosis of the bone in her leg and can only walk with difficulty. Vanessa's father, apart from medical considerations, thinks Piquette can in this way acquire some much needed rest as well as provide companionship for his daughter. Once there, Piquette is reproachful and morose, uncommunicative, and Vanessa is unable to connect.

One day Dr. MacLeod points out the loons at their habitat. He comments that the loons will soon disappear with the increasing development around the lake and ever more cottages. The key passage just quoted depicts Vanessa's gradual, then sudden, realization—a sort of epiphany for her—that the destiny of the loons as a vanishing species epitomizes the fate of Piquette and her social group, the Métis of Manawaka. This understanding occurs when some years later Vanessa learns from her mother of Piquette's squalid death back in the old Tonnerre shack after a fire breaks out and neither Piquette nor her children escape alive. "It seemed to me now," so the last sentence of the story, "that in some unconscious and totally unrecognized way, Piquette might have been the only one, after all, who had heard the crying of the loons" (*BH* 108). By extension, this phrasing wants to convey: Piquette has empathized with the *plaintive* ring in the crying of the loons which both expresses sorrow, mourning *and* a plaintiff's accusation directed at her circumstance in life. The cry is heightened by the element of *chilling mockery*, suggesting the Métis' inescapable doom.

At this point I wish to comment on a number of lexical meanings and significations of the term *loon*. While doing so, I propose to relate them tentatively to instances of the texts, especially those involving the Tonnerre family. The situations will come chiefly from *The Diviners* where the lives of the Tonnerres converge to form an integral part of Morag's existence. The most important of these relationships is obviously that of Morag and Jules and their daughter Pique.

In the Eleventh Edition of the *Encyclopaedia Britannica* (1910-11) the entry *Loon/Loom* has an interesting explanation, with a fitting reference to Icelandic *lómr* plus a variant form *lumme*. The author, Alfred Newton, in a special footnote has recourse to the philologist Walter W. Skeat, who is said to have observed that the form *lumme* "is probably connected with *lame*; . . . The signification of *loon*, a clumsy fellow, and metaphorically a simpleton, is obvious to anyone who has seen the attempt of the birds to which the name is given to walk." This somewhat moralistic anthropological comparison applied to this "almost wholly aquatic" species has been watered down in our current edition of the *Encyclopaedia Britannica* to this: "They have legs so far back on the body that walking is virtually impossible" (1034).

When we return to the story "The Loons" and take a closer look, we begin to be more appreciative of certain passages, non-committal as they seem. One such is the description of Piquette: "with her hoarse voice and her clumsy limping walk" (97). And again: "She was sitting on the swing, her lame leg held stiffly out" (99). Another description further on runs: "I thought it was probably her slow and difficult walking that held her back" (103). On the surface these passages make plain, realistic, naturalistic enough reading. They are convincingly denotative. In reality, however, these descriptions are part of a pattern of imagery carefully building up the sense of a fundamentally disabled being. What is being described is an inescapable existential state of mutilation which, in terms of the story, turns out to be literally fatal.

Seen in this light, when we find that the very first paragraph of "The Loons" tells us that *old* Jules Tonnerre had built the original small shack "some fifty years before, when he came back from Batoche with a bullet in his thigh, the year that Riel was hung and the voices of the Métis entered their long silence" (96), this mutilation has attained a historical and existential dimension. While anatomically the original wound is in keeping with the outline of the story, the clumsy metaphorical limp is the heritage of these *human* loons, and is as natural an attribute as the inherited clumsy gait of the water fowl who are unfit for land—consequently, who are out of their depth.

Next in this list is *loon* the *scamp, idler, lazy loon* (originally Scottish and Northern dialect usage); *a worthless person, a rogue, sluggard, boor, lout, clown*; an *untaught, ill-bred person*; *a strumpet, slut, slovenly person, harlot, concubine*. Some well-known colloquial phrases are: *wild as a loon, drunk as a loon, mad, crazy as a loon, homo stupidus, a simpleton*; we even find *a foreign loon*. That these instances and their colloquial usage have been fused with the entire semantics of *loony*, as in *loony bin*, is amply documented. The 1976 *OED Supplement* links *crazy, drunk as a loon*, directly with the "wild cry" of the loon "escaping from danger." Another example refers us appropriately to Laurence country proper. This is a reference in an 1880 publication titled *Trip to Manitoba*: "the weird cry of the loon diving."

A catalogue like this practically covers the semantic field of behavioural patterns sometimes attributed to a whole set of Canadian "fringe groups." Such groups may include various "ethnic" cultures that have not adjusted to the "modern" technological or bureaucratic versions of "mainstream" society. Native Canadians may be among such "fringe groups" that are not immediately upwardly mobile.

Next we have the phrase *lord and loon*, which stems from the legal system of feudal subordination. This term adds an interesting touch contextually: designated as chiefly Scottish or archaic, *loon* refers to "a man of low birth or condition," "a rascally or ruffianly servant, a groom, menial, varlet." This terminology would fit well the "peer and peasant, the lord and loon" relationship that historically characterizes the tensions between the fringe and WASP communities. The Morag Gunn/MacLeod families of the Manawaka series, and for that matter Margaret Laurence herself, cannot help identifying with the mainstream community *vis-à-vis* the marginalized Métis in these terms. The uneasy relationship proposed by these semantic considerations provides the tension and emotional attraction vital to the development of the Tonnerre/Gunn stories. I shall refrain from going into what this constellation might yield in terms of the Hegelian Master/Servant analyses and their application to the problems of class strife and class consciousness.

A more picturesque note is struck with the most recent lemmata in the list of *loon* entries (*OED Supplement* 1976): a) a style of close fitting casual trousers, *loon pants, loon trousers, velvet loons*; and b) *to loon*, "especially of young people: to spend one's leisure time in a pleasurable way, e.g. by dancing to popular music; to lie *about*, to wander *about*." Examples illustrating this contextual usage all come from the late sixties and the seventies, right up to 1974. This usage also includes colloquialisms where *looning, looners*, are applied to the popular music scene, performers and songsters, such as the "king looner [who] became a symbol of good fun and good time music"; also "children and the younger adults alike looning about in wonderful costumes."

This updates the semantic field to the time when the Manawaka cycle of novels was written and which constitutes much of the setting especially for *The Diviners* (1974). In the concluding sections, with the "Album" appendix in particular, Laurence maps out for Jules and his daughter Pique their roles as popular ballad writers and songsters, however tentatively embarked on. They integrate the family or ethnic lore into their lyrics. Thematically the content of these songs, as well as the impulse to create them, is incorporated in the characters' search for identity and self assertion.

When we reach the 1960s and '70s, however, times have changed. The new brand of individualistic and yet still tribally motivated *loons* and *looners* is beginning to move within the mainstream climate. I am referring to the "emancipated" lifestyles of the semi-domesticated counter-cultures of former decades—the hippies and the post-hippies. Cultural and social changes have made once-hereditary handicaps inconspicuous. What was formerly unconventional has become socially acceptable, and this includes an equation of Picaresque/migrant lives with intellectual flexibility. The protagonists of Laurence's novels become central to our search for basic human values. The course discovered for them, and by extension for the reader, becomes at once melancholic and pathetic, as well as optimistic and pragmatic. In a double-edged and parodic way almost, the "loony, looning about looners" are deploying talents that are simultaneously highly individualistic and traditional. Or, if we may appropriate for the topic one of Rudy Wiebe's formulas, they are becoming voices to be heard in "the full orchestra in our world of beautiful complexities" (Wiebe 143).

It is then comparatively easy to spot in Margaret Laurence's nonfictional prose essential ramifications of the *loon* semantics. Of a variety of such instances, let me point to one that is recognizably related to her causes of a civic or international scope. I refer to her article "Man of Our People" in *Heart of a Stranger*, where her introductory remarks strike a confessional and article of faith note which has "a great deal of relevance to my own life-view," with special attention drawn to "a relevance which is to be found in much of my work, . . . perhaps seen in its broadest sense in my novel, *The Diviners*" (227). Here Laurence evaluates George Woodcock's *Gabriel Dumont, The Métis Chief and His Lost World* (1975) and she describes her own sense of being captivated by what might be called Woodcock's dialectics in interweaving the Dumont/Riel complex.

Laurence's closing paragraphs of "Man of Our People" evoke the extended *loon* metaphor in two distinct ways. The first of these is the voice element. "Canadians . . . ," descendants of settlers, many of whom came as oppressed or dispossessed peoples, "must hear native peoples' voices and ultimately become part of them," for they speak, she continues, "of their rediscovered sense of self worth and their ability to tell and teach the things needed to be known" (235-36). Things which our consumer-oriented society has lost or discarded. The second way in which the loon metaphor is extended, and which converges with the first, is the environmentalist/conservationist stance. The Métis, via the legend of Riel and Dumont, are turned into an analogy of the endangered species and the Wretched of the Earth:

> We have largely forgotten how to live with, protect, and pay homage to our earth and the other creatures who share it with us—as witness the killing of rivers and

> lakes; the killing of the whales; . . . We have so much to learn and act upon, and time is getting short. Those other societies which existed before imperialism, industrialism, mass exploitation, and commercial greed were certainly far from ideal, nor can we return to them, but they knew about living in relationship to the land, and they may ultimately be the societies from whose values we must try to learn. (235)

Apart from some generalizations, Laurence's train of thought in some way invokes the "*human* creativity [that] has in it the quality of *re*-creation, of salvaging something with a human meaning out of the alienation of nature" (Frye 138).

The various word-games and usages I have brought up for the word *loon* through a variety of seemingly unrelated texts, both fictional and nonfictional, suggest another observation by Northrop Frye:

> . . . the words of multiple meanings that allow for puns, are all accidents, or, as philologists like to say "pure" coincidences; yet they make up a texture that enters into the mental processes of all native speakers of the language whether they are writers or not. (4)

I should like to qualify this even further, with the evoked semantic field of *loon* in the background. The uses of geographical distribution, familiar objects in nature, which have been referred to in relation to semantics, demonstrate a continual concern for the referential character of words. The dictionary lemmata of *loon* help to depersonalize and objectify experience and emotion as they occur in the story "The Loons." They serve as markers, trigonometrical points on the memory-map/-bank on the level of *Langue* as well as on the level of *Parole* when it comes to identifying particulars in the texture of our awareness—both of issues and "real messy people" who do not conform to mainstream social patterns. Objects at hand, in nature, "the smallest details of geography" for instance, Frye claims ". . . have become part of the map of our own imaginative world, whether we have ever seen [such objects as loons] or not" (218).

Speaking in terms of the W. Iser/R. Ingarden implications of the phenomenological school of hermeneutics, we might say it is due to "objective correlatives" or even "Concrete Universals" such as *loons* that a text exists "both as a positional force and a referential field. It must both found a new world unique at every instant and efface itself in the designation of familiar pre-existent reality" (Ray 56). As readers we start with the known by identifying familiar references. Such "experiential" reading synthesizes new objects out of previously experienced situations. What may or may not have been in Laurence the author a "private construct" of meanings, it is our "reflective" reading that recasts the narrative into a transparent, shared "conceptual structure" (Ray 57). That structure is shared by the lexical or socio-linguistic map of the regional speech community. The observation points of the contextual landscape that spring from the ramifications of the once central *loon* imagery appear as knots in the grid/network of a thematic texture that connects several otherwise independent books/stories. The *loon's* radiations into and from various textures display the dynamics of a "referential force" of the "fictional text's repertoire." That repertoire is "all the familiar territory within the text," which "incorporates a specific external reality into the text, and so offers the reader a definite frame of reference or invokes a definite range of past experience" (Iser 212).

It is a case in point of "the matter of implicit metaphor" when our "attention as we read is . . . going simultaneously in two directions, outward to the conventional or remembered meaning, inward to the specific meaning," as Frye says in *The Great Code* (57). In referential terms, Margaret Atwood has pointed to the imaginative act of concretization which in all the genres of the poetic is "rooted . . . in the inescapable concrete, both in image and in verbal usage" (xxxix). Margaret Laurence herself discusses this native "feel" for the familiar in her 1986 interview for *Border Crossings* when she and her interviewers are setting it off against Grove: "We don't live in the verbal landscape Grove describes," Laurence says:

> When I read Grove, I thought, "I don't recognize this terrain, I do not, it is not mine." And the reason is that it was *not* his. He came to Manitoba as an exile and he felt himself to be an exile all the time. It was my world, it was the world that gave me my sight . . . it was the world I knew intimately. (33)

In this sense Manitobans justly feel themselves to be among the first beneficiaries of the Laurence "unreal estate" which they can naturally identify with in the relative security of their "lighted lamps of home." The loons' nostalgic "Call of Canada" is then one type of shared ambiguity between Canadians. Yet for the international reader, the semantic field evoked here also has a certain air of recognition given an inkling for the English lingo. Loons and metaphors may limp—that is how they hobble their way into the mental map of understanding:

> You will not grasp what Language speaks—and what it has to tell us—if it does not reach out into and evoke the familiar, in order to be the mediator between the known and familiar and the very message of the text. (Gadamer 418)

Works Consulted

Arnason, David and Dennis Cooley. "Outcasting: A Conversation with Margaret Laurence about the World of Manawaka." *Border Crossings* 5.4 (1986): 32-35.

Atwood, Margaret. Introduction. *The New Oxford Book of Canadian Verse in English*. Toronto: Oxford U.P., 1982. xxvii-xxxix.

Cooley, Dennis, ed., *RePlacing*. Downsview: ECW Press, 1980.

A Dictionary of Americanisms. 4th ed. 1966.

A Dictionary of the Older Scottish Tongue. 1974.

Frye, Northrop. *The Great Code. The Bible and Literature*. Toronto: Academic Press, 1982.

__________. "The Motive for Metaphor." *The Educated Imagination*. Toronto: CBC, 1963. 1-11.

Gadamer, H.G. *Wahrheit und Methode*. Tübingen: MOHR, 1960.

Iser, Wolfgang. *The Act of Reading*. Baltimore: Johns Hopkins U.P., 1974.

Laurence, Margaret. *A Bird in the House*. 1963. Toronto: Seal Books, 1978.

__________. *Heart of a Stranger*. 1976. Toronto: Seal Books, 1980.

MURET Encyclopaedic English-German and German-English Dictionary. Berlin and New York, 1891.

Nabokov, Vladimir. *Speak, Memory. An Autobiography Revisited*. Rev. Ed. New York: Putnam Capricorn, 1970.

Newman, Peter C. Review of *The Apprentice's Tale*. *The Beaver* 67.3 (June-July 1987): 55-56.

Oxford American Dictionary. 1980.

Ray, William. *Literary Meaning. From Phenomenology to Deconstruction*. Oxford: Blackwell, 1984.

Rosenblatt, Louise M. *Literature as Exploration*. 1938. London, 1970.

van Herk, Aritha. "Mapping as Metaphor." *Zeitschrift der Gesellschaft für Kanada-Studien* 2 (1982).

Voltaire. *Oeuvres Historiques*. Ed. René Pomeau. Paris: Gallimard, 1957.

Webster's Third New International Dictionary. 1971.

Wiebe, Rudy. "One-stringed Lutes." *Journal of Commonwealth Literature* 19 (1984): 142-43.

Diana Brydon
University of British Columbia

Silence, Voice and the Mirror: Margaret Laurence and Women

My title suggests a double focus: Margaret Laurence writing about women, and women reading Margaret Laurence. I believe the female reader brings a perspective and expectations to a text that are different from those of the "ideal" reader we have been taught to try to emulate. Because her socialization as woman and as reader could conflict, she may be more attuned to similar tensions experienced by female characters within a text. Laurence herself has commented on this phenomenon:

> . . . some of my work, particularly *The Fire-Dwellers*, received some real put-downs from a number of male reviewers. They didn't even say it was a bad novel; it was just that if anybody like Stacey existed, they just would rather not know. And the other is . . . this is not done so much any more but at one time people used to say as a compliment that a woman writer wrote like a man. Well, this I used to find infuriating. I write like a human being, one hopes, of course with a woman's point

> of view. I am a woman. But whoever said about a male novelist, he is a man novelist, or worse, a gentleman novelist? (Gibson 200)

Laurence writes from a woman's point of view. What follows is one woman's reading of the women in Margaret Laurence's fiction.

Character is the central element in Laurence's writing. She says:

> I always start with the main character or, as it may be, characters. Usually there are a number of people who have been inhabiting my head for a number of years before I begin on a novel, and their dilemmas grow out of what they are, where they come from. (Gibson 195)

She explains:

> I take on, for the time I'm writing, the *persona* of the character, and I am trying to make a kind of direct connection with this person, not to manipulate them but to listen to them, to try and feel my way into their skull in such a way that I respond in the writing the way they would respond, which of course naturally is both me and not me: this is where it gets so peculiar, because it's aspects of myself and yet it's not totally me, it's them as well. They exist in their own right. (Cameron 103)

Laurence is interested in human situations and in both male and female characters. Yet one cannot speak of Margaret Laurence's fiction without focussing on her women. The Manawaka novels centre on female characters and are told from their individual points of view. Clara Thomas writes that "As studies of 'Women in Our Times' these novels are stunningly authentic" (Novels 65). Taken together, they provide a composite portrait of Canadian women in the middle of this century. One can speak interchangeably of the Manawaka world or of the Manawaka women of Margaret

Laurence. It is the women who reflect and refract that world; that world which provides them with the material for their monologic dialogues with self that are the novels. *The Stone Angel* is Hagar's story. *A Jest of God* is Rachel's. *The Fire-Dwellers* is Stacey's. *A Bird in the House* is Vanessa's. *The Diviners* is Morag's. Each woman tells her own story in her own voice and each is very different, yet their shared experience of the condition of being a woman colours all their stories with similar thematic concerns.

The concerns of Laurence's women have been identified by feminist theorists as characteristic of how middle-class white women experience and write about the world in twentieth-century North America. In this paper I will concentrate on three of the most striking ways in which this particular female experience shapes Laurence's narratives.

The first elaborates on the first-person point of view so central to these fictions. Each of Laurence's narrators is in search of her own voice, troubled by the ambiguous relations between language and silence, speech and thought, words and power. Like many North American writers, Laurence uses "women's exclusion from language" as one of her themes (Irvine 9). Laurence notes of her writing:

> I was dealing with a lot of the stuff Women's Lib is talking about right now. But at the time I was doing it I didn't realize how widespread some of these feelings were. I used to be surprised when I got letters from women saying, 'Right on.' My generation of women came to a lot of the same conclusions, but they did it in isolation: you weren't supposed to say those things out loud, to question the assumption that the woman's only role was that of housewife. (Atwood 37)

These novels take place within the narrators' heads. They speak little of what they think. The roles assigned them as women require a certain kind of speech and more listening. Like Vanessa, they are "professional listener[s]" (*BH* 11). Their stories reveal their entrapment in these assigned roles and their efforts to find a way out of them through developing a new way of using words. Like Morag when she breaks with Brooke, these women realize that they do not know the sound of their own voices. Morag's moment of self-realization when she confronts Brooke's male insistence that she is essentially determined by her biology is paradigmatic. He tells her she is hysterical and asks: "Are you due to menstruate?" (*Div* 256). In response, "Morag stands absolutely silent. *I do not know the sound of my own voice. Not yet, anyhow*" (*Div* 257). Only when she has realized that lack can she hesitantly begin to search for what she has lost, the "private and fictional words" (*Div* 453) that will free her into speech. Although she and Vanessa are the only writers among the Manawaka women, each woman must go through a similar process of discovering her own voice. Hagar confesses her story to Murray F. Lees and blesses Marvin; Rachel tells her mother they must leave Manawaka and writes her sister; Stacey finally has an honest confrontation with Mac; Vanessa presumably has written *A Bird in the House*, as Morag has created *The Diviners*.

Secondly, although each novel focusses on a central female character in search of her identity, that identity is ultimately determined by her relations with others. As feminist theorists have noted, the female hero, unlike the traditional male hero, does not separate herself from others to mature. Instead, she defines herself in relation to others. But Laurence shifts the focus of the traditional female story from the heterosexual couple to the parent/child relation (Aitken 118). In Laurence's fiction, the mother/child relation is dominant, even for a spinster like Rachel. The other side of this positive sense of connection to others, however, is a world of powerless entrapment. All of Laurence's women wish to escape their small town and their dependence on husbands, fathers or grandfathers, yet they have limited financial freedom because as women their options are even more curtailed than their men's. The need to escape and the need to re-affiliate are equally strong.

Yet these novels also create alternative female worlds that counter the dominance of the patriarchal family. Grandfather Connor flaunts his economic power, but his wife has a stronger emotional power, and his daughters create an alternative female domain from which he is excluded but which nurtures and sustains his granddaughter Vanessa. Rachel's most intense and ambivalent relations are finally, surprisingly, not with Nick, but with her mother, her sister Stacey, and her friend Calla. Perhaps the dominant relationship in Hagar's life has been her rivalry with No-Name Lottie; certainly it had a stronger impact on her behaviour than her love for Bram or John. Morag's lasting lifelong relationship is with her friend Ella. Through Ella, she is embraced by the supportive female world of the Gersons. Stacey, again surprisingly, given that she is the housewife, seems the only central female character denied the warmth or rivalry of lifelong female connections. She fails her neighbour, Tess, and Tess attempts suicide, because both are cut off from these sustaining alternative female worlds. Tess's Polyglam Superware party offers only a false camaraderie. Money and things bring these women together, but silence continues to hold them apart.

Thirdly, as in the paradigmatic fairy-tale "Snow White" and the Victorian poem "The Lady of Shalott," each of these women has her own special relationship with the mirror, which underlines visually the dichotomy between role and real definitions of the self, between what one sees and what one feels, between what one wants others to see and what one wants to see oneself. The guilt and rebellion felt by each of these women as she wavers between saying "I can't" and "I won't," between apologizing and affirming, between claiming innocence and embracing responsibility, is often focussed by her encounters with the mirror. The mirror guarantees one kind of identity while annihilating others. It can reflect external appearances or direct the watcher into internal realities. But always it is closely linked to silence and it encourages the female protagonist to see herself as her chief work of art, turning her away from verbalized self-expression and communication toward solipsism.

1. "Nothing that can be spoken"

In *A Jest of God*, Rachel thinks: "There isn't much to say about myself, nothing that can be spoken" (96). This is the paradox of Rachel's life; there is so much to be longed for in private thought, yet so little that can be spoken. And ironically, it is this very failure to speak that condemns the silent to continue in lonely suffering. *A Jest of God* allows its readers to hear what cannot be spoken: Rachel's voice in all its ambiguities of fear and longing. There is a whole novel's worth of things to say about herself, yet very little of it can be spoken aloud because of her fear of what people might think, of their gossip and their judgement. In this way, Rachel resembles the character of Lilac in Morag Gunn's first novel *Spear of Innocence*. Brooke believes the novel "suffers from having a protagonist who is non-verbal, that is, she talks a lot, but she can't communicate very well." Morag responds that this "was part of the problem" (246). The professional male reader, Brooke, is blind to the woman's point of view, to her *way* of saying. All Laurence's novels seek to attune their readers to woman's hesitant attempts at speech in a male-dominated medium within a male-dominated world. As Coral Ann Howells suggests of contemporary Canadian women's writing in general: "heroism is redefined in these fictions, for these are stories about inner adventures which are often invisible to other people" (5).

From the outside male point of view, Rachel seems a Sphinx or Mona Lisa (*BH* 12). But from within, her apparent mystery becomes a mesh of fears about her inadequacy as a human being. She hears her very thoughts as an echo of her mother's voice (9) and is outwardly silent because she never knows what to say (10). When her own voice does speak, it seems disembodied and uncontrollable, an appalling transgression of a deeply held taboo:

> Silence. I can't stay. I can't stand it. I really can't. Beside me, the man moans gently, moans and stirs, and moans—
>
> *That voice*!
>
> Chattering, crying, ululating, the forbidden transformed cryptically to nonsense, dragged from the crypt, stolen and shouted, the shuddering of it, the fear, the breaking, the release, the grieving—
>
> Not Calla's voice. Mine. Oh my God. Mine. The voice of Rachel. (37)

This incident encapsulates the story of the book: when the silence about sex and death becomes unbearable the repressed emerges in uncontrollable and unrecognizable form, as nonsense. The crypt made cryptic. Rachel is appalled by the sound of her own voice, revealing all the emotions she has held hidden inside for so long. Loss of control is associated with the release of speech. Others may use speech to control and calm—the "preacher's voice is creamy as mayonnaise" (34)—but for Rachel to speak is to risk blurting "out something unpardonable" (43). Decent women should not know about such things. Everything that most occupies Rachel's mind—all the important questions about life and values and death—are dismissed as "not a subject for discussion" (40).

The novel repeats the same pattern throughout. Rachel tells her mother nothing about her first date with Nick, and then shocks herself by what she is goaded into saying: "I can't believe myself, that I could have said what I did" (64). And again with Nick, she blurts out " 'I hate living here.' This is the last thing in the world I ever intended to say" (64), she thinks to herself immediately afterwards. Obedient silence leads to rebellious speech followed by guilty self-recrimination. All these unclaimed voices speak through her—the official teacher's, her mother's, her sister's, her own abortive attempts at self-expression—until finally, under the anaesthetic, she speaks in a voice that seems truly and finally hers: "*I am the mother now*" (160).

Stacey, her married sister, outwardly so different, lives through the same pattern. Her small talk serves the same function as Rachel's awkward silences: both deny speech to their thoughts, to what their town has taught them must not be spoken. Whereas Rachel's outburst occurs during a religious service of a socially suspect denomination, Stacey's takes place at a business party. She tries to silence herself: "Stacey, girl, shut your trap" (*FD* 108), babbles what sounds like drunken nonsense: "I mean infrusion, that's what I mean but I guess I shouldn't have brought it up" (108), and finally decisively interrupts the polite formalities with a bawdy joke (109). Her husband Mac reprimands her: "Dry up, Stacey. You've said enough tonight" (110).

Throughout *The Fire-Dwellers*, Stacey's refrain is "Talk to me": "Katie—talk to me. Mac, talk to me" (121). Throughout *A Jest of God*, Rachel's refrain is "*Nick—listen—*" (160). Each seeks acknowledgement through speech yet each fears speech as much as she fears silence. Stacey asks Luke: "can you imagine what it's like to live in the same house with somebody who doesn't talk or who can't or else won't and I don't know which reason it could be" (197), but when Mac tries to speak, "Stacey cannot say anything to enable him to speak, because she is afraid of what he will say" (237). These are the paradoxes all Laurence's women inhabit.

In *A Jest of God*, Calla's canary never does learn to sing, but in *The Fire-Dwellers* Stacey's little girl, Jen, named for her aunt Rachel and silent throughout the novel (to her mother's perturbation), does find her voice at the novel's end: "Hi, Mum. Want tea?" (299). This revelation parallels her parents' establishing better communication within their marriage and her aunt's discovery, miles away in another book, of her own voice. The letter Rachel writes at the end of her story arrives at the end of Stacey's story, bringing the two of them together once more, however ambivalently.

Hagar, in *The Stone Angel*, seems to have the opposite problem. Refusing the self-censorship that is the traditional role assigned to women, she speaks without thinking, just like a man. She proudly models herself on her father, rejecting the meekness of her mother who died giving birth to her. She refuses to play her mother to comfort her dying brother Dan: "To play at being her—it was beyond me" (25). Modelling herself on her father's rigidity, she is "unable to bend enough." Her father encourages her unbending nature, until she crosses him, when he disowns her. An overheard conversation between her father and Auntie Doll makes her second-class status as a woman clear: "Smart as a whip, she is, that one. If only she'd been—" (14). The gap here clearly signifies male, taking on more force because it remains unsaid, an unattainable impossibility for Hagar. Her identity comes from being his daughter, his property, as she realizes when she returns home from finishing school. He looks her over, and nods and nods "as though I were a thing and his" (43). Although she tries, she can never be his inheritor, his replica; she can only be his property. Yet she must forfeit even her status as Jason Currie's daughter on her marriage to Bram Shipley. She marries Bram thinking she can confer her father's status on him, forgetting that a woman's status, in the society Laurence depicts, depends on her husband's.

With no money or position of her own, she finds herself with nothing left of her old identity but her sharp tongue. When she tells Bram she is leaving him, he looks at her and says: "I got nothing to say, Hagar. It's you that's done the saying" (142). The tragedy is that she has never said what she felt or needed, only what she knew her father or her community would have expected her to say. The entire novel ruminates over what she comes to see as "the incommunicable years" (296). The testy, complaining voice has become her own, and speaks without her now: "I hear my accusing voice and I'm ashamed. But it won't stop" (274). She realizes: "I go on speaking in the same way, always" (296). But just before her death, she surprises herself by honestly confessing her fear to Marvin. She wonders: "What possessed me? I think it's the first time in my life I've ever said such a thing. Shameful. Yet somehow it is a relief to speak it. What can he say, though?" (303-04). What he says amounts to asking for her blessing, and she finds the courage now to give what she had withheld from Dan—the lie of a mother's love: "You've been good to me, always. A better son than John" (304). When it is spoken, she thinks of it as "a lie—yet not a lie, for it was spoken at least and at last with what may perhaps be a kind of love" (307).

Hagar assumes the male prerogative of speaking her mind, but pays the price: a lonely life, without her men. Only Marvin, whom she takes for granted, remains with her. The sole employment she can find is as a housekeeper, for a man whose work reminds her of her female status as an object to be traded by men. She is fascinated and horrified by his stories of the Chinese brides smuggled into the country in the holds of his ship. He would "pack the females like tinned shrimp in the lower hold, and if the Immigration men scented the hoax, the false bottom was levered open, and the women plummeted. . . . And Mr. Oatley would shrug and smile, begging my laughter and my approbation. And I'd oblige, for who could help it?" (156). Her job requires her to play the obliging female role that she had refused to play with her father and her husband. She plays it now for her son John's sake, but he fails to appreciate the sacrifice.

Although Hagar blames her problems on herself, in the end, the reader can see that the Manawaka world offered little scope to her energies and intelligence. Certainly, she carried her chains within her, internalizing her society's judgements about what was and was not proper, but even if she could have escaped such indoctrination, there was little she might have done beyond being a better wife and mother, and hers was not a nature suited to such roles.

Hagar's story may be put in focus by Grandfather Connor's in *A Bird in the House*. Like Hagar, he is cranky and irascible, but unlike her, he wields real power. Hagar's men are free to ignore or leave her, and they do. She wields emotional power only. Grandfather Connor's power is more absolute. His wife, his daughters, and his granddaughter have nowhere else to go. They long to escape, but the only form of escape open to them is through silence and finally death, for his wife, or through voluntary commitment to another male protector, for his daughters. The community believes with Grandmother MacLeod that "a family whose men are gone is no family at all" (111). When her husband dies, Vanessa's mother Beth must move back under her father's control, knowing she may never escape it again: "Maybe I can't get out. But they [her children] will" (186). Vanessa "was frantic to get away . . . [but] did not see how it was going to be possible" (202). Her mother finds the money to send her to university. She tells Vanessa:

> "When I was your age . . . I got the highest marks in the province in my last year of high school. I guess I never told you that. I wanted to go to college. Your grandfather didn't believe in education for women, then." (203)

When Grandfather Connor speaks, everyone is forced to listen. He has the privilege of free speech. The women can only speak covertly. Vanessa writes: "I felt, as so often in the Brick House, that my lungs were in danger of exploding, that the pressure of silence would become too great to be borne. . . . But I did not say anything. I was not that stupid" (66). Silence is a survival technique mastered young. She listens to the adults and writes her stories, finding her freedom in the silent and private world of writing. Her family training in reticence makes it hard for her, as for all of Laurence's characters, to communicate her feelings. With Chris, she finds "I could not speak even the things I knew" (151). It is the same with her father: "I wanted to speak in some way that would be more poignant and comprehending than anything of which my mother could possibly be capable. But I did not know how" (93). What she finds instead is that, as she puts it, "my own voice carried some disturbing echoes of my grandfather's" (159). Twenty years later, she thinks: "I remembered saying things to my children that my mother had said to me, the clichés of affection, perhaps inherited from her mother" (207). Like all Laurence's women, Vanessa discovers that her personal voice is an amalgam of the voices of her family, resisted yet finally claimed on her own terms of being.

2. *"I am the mother now"*

"I am the mother now" (*JG* 160)—Rachel's words under anaesthetic, repeated in full consciousness later when she recognizes her mother's need for her reassurance, represent the claiming of responsibility that all Laurence's women come to when they have sorted through their lives. Silence hurts them because it represents their impotence, their powerlessness to reach out to others to establish the connections they need. Many of their men experience a similar impotence when it comes to human relationships, because men and women alike share a common Puritan heritage of repression in the Manawaka world. But the men have outlets denied the women, chiefly through their work and their ability to command attention, as Grandfather Connor does, by reminding their dependents who pays the bills. Wondering why her grandfather seldom drove his car, Vanessa speculates naughtily that "perhaps he had never grown accustomed to the fact that it could not be controlled by shouting" (177). Many of the mothers in Laurence's novels learn how to control through other means. The subtle emotional manipulations of Grandmother MacLeod, Hagar and Mrs. Cameron are no less tyrannical than Grandfather Connor's more direct insistence, but they are different. Their indirect methods derive from their weaker positions; their insistence derives from their desperation: for them, family dominance is all. But the

claiming of motherhood that Rachel comes to at the end of *A Jest of God* is not so much the need to dominate as the recognition that she has responsibilities beyond herself. After a book of silently begging others to listen she prays at the end "*Make me to hear . . . Make me to hear joy and gladness, that the bones which Thou hast broken may rejoice*" (174). Journeying with her mother, now her "elderly child" (174), toward her sister and an unknown future, she is prepared to start listening herself as well as crying to be heard. The egotistical child is growing into the nurturing mother.

Stacey goes through a similar metamorphosis from the opposite direction, thinking "I'd like to talk to my sister. I'd like to write to her. I'd like to tell her how I feel about everything" (*FD* 277). She has listened to others too long; she needs to tell her own story now, but in telling it she remains the mother. She invites her father-in-law into her home, prepares to welcome her mother and sister to Vancouver, and resolves to accept her own aging more gracefully: "I won't be twenty-one again" (308). More importantly, perhaps, she decides not to force her need to verbalize everything onto her husband and sons. They can express their connectedness in other ways. In the car after Duncan's near drowning, Mac says:

> Ian?
> Yeh?
> You did fine.
> Stacey looks at the two unbending necks in the front seat.
> —That's the most Mac will ever be able to say. They're not like me, either of them. They don't want to say it in full technicolour and intense detail. And that's okay, I guess. Ian gets the message. It's his language, too. I wish it were mine. All I can do is accept that it is a language, and that it works, at least sometimes. And maybe it's mine more than I like to admit. Whatever I think that I think of it, it's the one I most use." (295-96)

This is how all Laurence's characters communicate, in a speech "gapped with silences" (*JG* 112), yet with the same resolve to make it work for them, in affirming their interrelatedness to one another.

Rachel and Stacey live in their minds, talking most often through what Rachel terms the "private telephone of silence" (*JG* 159). Paradoxically, each talks to others most often when alone. As Rachel puts it:

> I talk to him, when he is not here, and tell him everything I can think of, everything that has ever happened, and how I feel and for awhile it seems to me that I am completely known to him, and then I remember I've only talked to him like that when I'm alone. He hasn't heard and doesn't know. (*JG* 122)

This kind of silent talk intensifies her loneliness and heightens her isolation. Stacey's zanier array of voices work to the same end, as do Hagar's triggered recollections of scenes from the past. In contrast, Morag and Vanessa take similar silent dialogues with others and transform them into fictional works. As people they meet the same silences, but as writers they can use them to help their readers experience and understand them.

Vanessa, a mother herself, returns to Manawaka to make her peace with her dead ancestors at the end of her story. Hagar makes peace with her descendants at the end of hers. Family ties are important to all these women. They have formed the environment in which they have been shaped and misshapen; they represent the community in microcosm. But the biological family in Laurence's world is superseded by the larger human family. In each novel it is a stranger, not a family member, who enables the central character to come to terms with herself and her heritage. Murray F. Lees acts as Hagar's unofficial confessor, Luke Ventura as Stacey's, Nick Kazlik as Rachel's. Chris, Piquette and Harvey Shinwell open avenues of understanding for Vanessa; Royland and A-Okay for Morag. *The Diviners* best embodies Laurence's vision of human community as an interrelatedness transcending mere blood ties. In adopting Hagar's clan motto for her own, Morag thinks "But adoption, as who should know better than Morag, is possible" (432). This act connects the first to the last of the Manawaka novels to show how the deforming patriarchal heritage of Hagar's world may be creatively transformed through Morag's matriarchal imagination from a negative to a positive force. Similarly, whereas Hagar had held to her father's rigid claiming of an old-world inheritance, Morag moves from Christie's initially liberating but still male-oriented tales of Piper Gunn to discover her own independent female model in the pioneer writer Catharine Parr Traill.

In Laurence's fiction, taking on motherhood means taking on responsibility, not just for one other life, but for the continuity and development of humanity. All her central women characters seek that loving connection to others that is symbolized by the mother-child bond. Fran Brady's abortions represent her hurt at being cut off from that kind of love, and from the ability to provide it, affirming motherhood as ideal even as she rejects it in actuality. Just as *The Diviners* affirms the indirect lines of inheritance transmitted through adoption, so *A Jest of God* affirms the symbolic rather than the literal value of motherhood in Laurence's fiction. It is fitting, rather than ironic, that Rachel, the only central female character denied literal motherhood, should conclude her story with the recognition: "*I am the mother now*," for motherhood in these novels provides an alternative definition of adulthood to that traditionally found in male fictions of development. Instead of affirming independence from the claims of others, as male heroes tend to do, these women learn to accept and even affirm the claims of others on them. They find independence in affiliation rather than in separation, but they choose their affiliations.

3. "I can't succeed in avoiding my eyes in the mirror" (*JG* 20)

For all Laurence's women, the relation with the mirror is an ambivalent one. Their reflection in the mirror confirms their reality while reminding them that the image in the mirror fails to match their ideal selves. The mirror provides confirmation of selfhood and scope for self-flagellation. Hagar, Morag and Rachel each feels with Stacey that "I'm not what I may appear to be" (*FD* 73). And I'm not what I should be. Laurence suggests that *The Fire-Dwellers* was written in rebellion against the images of women the mirrors of contemporary literature provided them. She said:

> I was fed up with the current fictional portraits of women of my generation—middle-aged mums either being presented as glossy magazine types, perfect, ever-loving and incontestably contented, or else as sinister and spiritually cannibalistic monsters determined only to destroy their men and kids by hypnotic means. (Ten Years 22)

Stacey too is fed up with these images, yet reads compulsively, matching herself against the two images, and concluding from her failure to fit either one that there must be something the matter with her. The novel's first page draws attention to the centrality of the mirror in Stacey's life:

> The full-length mirror is on the bedroom door. Stacey sees images reflected there, distanced by the glass like humans on TV, less real than real and yet more sharply focused because isolated and limited by a frame. (*FD* 3)

The mirror tells her that she is gaining weight and growing old; it does not tell of her desires, her memories and her fears for the future. It frames her physical appearance as if this were her only reality. She knows that neither her literal image in the mirror, nor the articles written for housewives like her reflect her own complex reality. Nonetheless, she can't stop checking herself in these mirrors, and she hasn't the courage to challenge their version of reality with an alternative one of her own, as Morag and Vanessa eventually do. Her dreams mirror her fears that for wanting more than she has she is a monster, a Medusa:

> The rain forest is thick, matted, overgrown. . . . She has to continue, bringing what she is carrying with her. The thing is bleeding from the neck stump, but that cannot be helped. The severed head spills only blood, nothing else. She has tunneled at last through the undergrowth. Now she has the right to look. She holds it up in front of her. How is it that she can see it? What is she seeing it with? That is the question. The head she has been carrying is of course none but hers. (124)

The Medusa, the horrific severed head of a woman in ancient Greek myth, had the power to turn to stone all who looked upon her. Stacey's Medusa dream is a variation of the stone angel motif in the first of the Manawaka novels. Each represents woman's fear of the power of her own desires in a society that forbids them expression.

Like Stacey, Hagar needs her mirrors. Of her belongings she says, "If I am not somehow contained in them and in this house, something of all change caught and fixed here, then I do not know where I am to be found at all" (*SA* 36). However, her memory and her will see beyond the physical appearance in the mirror to her sense of her essential childhood self, a self Stacey has reluctantly left behind her: "when I look in my mirror and beyond the changing shell that houses me, I see the eyes of Hagar Currie, the same dark eye as when I first began to remember and to notice myself" (38). This sense of self survives old age as it survived the forced recognition of herself as an egg woman to others. Looking in the mirror after that discovery, Hagar thinks: "The face—a brown and leathery face that wasn't mine. Only the eyes were mine, staring as though to pierce the lying glass and get beneath to some truer image, infinitely distant" (133). Finally, the encounter with Murray F. Lees provides that truer image, in a setting where "the grubby glass windows of its wheelhouse catching our one taper's worth of light and glinting as though a mirror were set into the night" (232) establishes the symbolic environment for the mirroring of Hagar's self.

In *A Jest of God*, Rachel's mirrors reflect the extreme subjectivity of her perspective on everything. She comments: "In the hall mirror I can see this giraffe woman" (69), "And when I turn around I can see myself in the mirror, not quite see but almost, the silver fishwhite of arms, the crane of a body, gaunt metal or gaunt bird" (101). Rachel's mirrors are all distorting mirrors:

> I can see myself reflected dimly, like the negative of a photograph, in the wide glass of display windows. . . . As in the distorting mirrors at a fair, I'm made to look even taller than I am. I have to pass myself again and again, and see a thin streak of a person, like the stroke of a white chalk on a blackboard. (30)

She recognizes that she herself is the mirror, generating these distorted images of herself when she puzzles over Nick's final silence: "Maybe he thought I'd splinter like a shattered mirror, create some unlucky scene, scatter sharp fragments which he could only stand and look at with embarrassment. I wouldn't have" (133).

Physical mirrors are less important to Morag and Vanessa because they have the power of creating their own mirrors through words, mirrors which reflect more than surface appearances or societal prescriptions for feminine behaviour. Most of Laurence's women are resisting readers of the traditional male stories, but they can't all shape their own stories in the alternative patterns they might wish. Stacey can't accept her condescending male professor's view that

Clytemnestra was clearly to blame for the murder of her husband Agamemnon. He easily discounts what to Stacey is the most important element in the tragedy, the fact that Agamemnon murdered their daughter to facilitate his war. Stacey's female reading counters his male reading, but he has all the power and authority of the establishment behind him and she can only retreat: "Yeh well I guess you must know Dr. Thorne. Sorry" (*FD* 32). Morag engages in a similar losing debate with male authority when she addresses a paradox in Donne that the experts on his metaphysical paradoxes had missed. She recognizes that he can be "terrific" but notes that he can also be "cruel." Brooke is puzzled, and Morag explains:

> "Well, like, 'For God's sake hold your tongue and let me love.' That's a very cruel line. Supposing the lady had been able to write poetry—I mean, you wonder what she might have said of *him*."
>
> "You would not take it kindly, Miss Gunn, to be asked to hold your tongue?"
>
> Laughter from class. Morag's face feels unpleasantly warm—does it show?
>
> "No. No, I would not." (*Div* 191)

In marrying this teacher, Morag knows she must learn to silence the voicing of her own perspective. She thinks: "Words haunt her, but she will become unhaunted now, forevermore" (202). Initially, she is willing to sacrifice words to the man, but this proves to be a vow she cannot keep. Forced to choose, she finally chooses words and the freedom to mirror the reality she perceives. When Brooke wonders whether her first character, Lilac, "expresses anything which we haven't known before," Morag admits, "No. She doesn't. But *she* says it. That is what is different" (246-47). Here finding a voice and shattering the mirrors that have confined women to passive roles come together in the female artist's insistence that her books will mirror female experience as voiced and shaped by women.

In *Woman's Consciousness, Man's World*, Sheila Rowbotham writes that

> The prevailing social order stands as a great resplendent hall of mirrors. It owns and occupies the world as it is and the world as it is seen and heard. . . . In order to create an alternative an oppressed group must at once shatter the self-reflecting world which encircles it and, at the same time, project its own image onto history. (27)

Morag dramatically shatters the mirror-image Brooke has held up for her to emulate, refusing to continue going to the hairdresser and refusing to answer to his belittling term of endearment, "Little One." In writing Lilac's story, from Lilac's perspective, she is projecting the self-image of an oppressed group onto history. Marian Engel notes that "Rachel, Hagar, Morag and Stacey are all women who have been propagandized to believe that 'Woman' is a different sort of creature than they find her to be" (220). Society's mirror of "Woman" clashes with the images these women see when they look in their own mirrors. Initially they try to force their own mirror images to match Society's—Stacey through the banana diet, Morag through imitating the "ladies" in her community, Hagar through trying to maintain the standards taught her at finishing school, and Rachel through trying to evade her eyes in the mirror—because in Laurence, the eyes always reveal the truth about a person's inner identity. In the end, however, each of these characters comes to terms with the disparity between what she sees in her own mirror—what her eyes reveal—and what Society has told her she should be seeing. Finally, each woman shatters the societal mirror to project her own image onto the world around her and to begin to speak, however tentatively, in her own voice.

The Manawaka women are socially constituted by a specific discourse: that of small-town Puritanical Anglo-Scots Canada. Its contradictions tear them apart even as they give them their specific identities. Forbidden speech, they generate a torrent of words. Locked in the private selves assigned them by liberal humanist discourse, they nonetheless break out of that privacy to define their various senses of selfhood through their relations with others. Given a public identity by their mirrors, they prove elusive, evading the mirror's reflection for reflections generated by rebellion and desire. These women live in process, through growth, change and discovery. The endings of their stories leave them in flux, with provisional resolutions established by a greater sense of potential yet to be released or of further metamorphoses yet to be imagined. Laurence's women are shaped by their town but they are not defeated. Their strength and imagination survive to inspire further generations.

The reader leaves these novels remembering the voices: Hagar remembering, Rachel begging, Stacey worrying, Vanessa re-ordering and Morag re-creating. She is struck by the individual ways in which each character reaches out to others: Hagar mourning her lost men, Rachel yearning for her lost children, Stacey coping with a world whose demands are too much for her, Vanessa escaping to return in imagination, and Morag divining the future from the past. Hagar challenges her mirrors, Rachel evades them, Stacey anxiously consults them, Vanessa ignores them and Morag refashions them. Unlike the work of many of her North American contemporaries, Laurence's writing is remarkably free of anger. Her books give ordinary women their voices back. They reach out to their readers to establish a sense of community. And in claiming full humanity for all her female characters, her novels challenge the stereotypes that have limited women to preordained and constricting roles.

Works Consulted

Aitken, Johan Lyall. *Masques of Morality: Females in Fiction.* Toronto: The Women's Press, 1987.

Atwood, Margaret. "Face to Face." *Margaret Laurence.* Ed. W.H. New. Toronto: McGraw-Hill Ryerson, 1977. 33-40.

Cameron, Donald. "Margaret Laurence: The Black Celt Speaks of Freedom." *Conversations with Canadian Novelists, Part One.* Toronto: Macmillan, 1973. 86-115.

Demetrakopoulos, Stephanie A. "Laurence's Fiction: A Revisioning of Feminine Archetypes." *Canadian Literature* 93 (Summer 1982): 42-57.

Engel, Marian. "It's the Grit. Laurence Is Unforgettable Because She Is Us." *Margaret Laurence.* Ed. W.H. New. Toronto: McGraw-Hill Ryerson, 1977. 219-21.

Gibson, Graeme. "Margaret Laurence." *Eleven Canadian Novelists.* Toronto: Anansi, 1973. 181-208.

Howells, Coral Ann. *Private and Fictional Words: Canadian Women Novelists of the 1970s and 1980s.* London: Methuen, 1987.

Irvine, Lorna. *Sub / Version.* Toronto: ECW, 1986.

Laurence, Margaret. *A Bird in the House.* Toronto: McClelland & Stewart, 1974.

__________. *The Diviners.* 1974. Toronto: Bantam, 1975.

__________. *The Fire-Dwellers.* 1969. Toronto: McClelland & Stewart, 1973.

__________. *A Jest of God.* Toronto: McClelland & Stewart, 1966.

__________. "Sources." *Margaret Laurence.* Ed. W.H. New. Toronto: McGraw-Hill Ryerson, 1977. 12-16.

__________. *The Stone Angel.* 1964. Toronto: McClelland & Stewart, 1968.

__________. "Ten Years' Sentences." *Margaret Laurence.* Ed. W.H. New. Toronto: McGraw-Hill Ryerson, 1977. 17-23.

New, W.H., ed. *Margaret Laurence.* Toronto: McGraw-Hill Ryerson, 1977.

Rooke, Constance. "A Feminist Reading of *The Stone Angel.*" *Canadian Literature* 93 (Summer 1982): 26-41.

Rowbotham, Sheila. *Woman's Consciousness, Man's World.* Harmondsworth: Penguin, 1973.

Thomas, Clara. *The Manawaka World of Margaret Laurence.* Toronto: McClelland & Stewart, 1976.

__________. "The Novels of Margaret Laurence." *Margaret Laurence.* Ed. W.H. New. Toronto: McGraw-Hill Ryerson, 1977. 55-65.

Per Seyersted
University of Oslo

Afterword

The Final Days: Margaret Laurence and Scandinavia

WHEN I TOLD Margaret Laurence in 1982 that the 1979 Norwegian translation of *The Stone Angel* had just been reprinted in 85,000 copies (which would correspond to 500,000 in a country with the population of Canada), she could hardly believe it. Norwegian reviewers had praised the book when the first printing (2000 copies) appeared, and when the leading Norwegian book club now sent it to its members, they received it equally warmly.

This was most likely why Norma Edwards was told, when she was planning to take her wonderful one-woman show, "The Women of Margaret Laurence," to Europe, that there would be interest for it in Scandinavia, especially Norway. And indeed, in Oslo, a city smaller than Edmonton or Winnipeg, Norma Edwards had very good houses for her three performances, and both audiences and theatre critics were enthusiastic. This was in 1983; had she made the tour a year later, she would probably have gone on to Sweden, because by then *The Stone Angel* had been published in that country as well and there, too, been favourably reviewed. Soon thereafter, the book appeared also in Denmark.

It is not surprising that Scandinavians should be interested in Canada in general: geographically we are much alike; we share many of the same values, and we have in common many of the problems felt by countries living next door to a superpower. As for *The Stone Angel*, what the Scandinavian critics had to say was that it is a great and moving novel, written in a forceful, concrete language, with a technique that enables us to see Hagar both from within and without, and that the author makes Hagar, even with her self-destructive pride and her misused life, into a character that inspires and stimulates the reader with her fighting spirit, her will to live, and her grim humour.

Personally I would add that through her art in *The Stone Angel*, Laurence communicates genuine, deeply felt truths about the human condition, presented in an honest, direct, unaffected way. And I am convinced that everyone who had the privilege to know her would say that these words also applied to the author herself: she was honest and direct; she had warmth and kindness, and she had a genuine interest in people and in the world in general.

When I was invited in 1982 to visit Laurence in Lakefield (a common acquaintance had written to her that I was teaching Canadian Studies in Norway and was now touring Canada, and that I would not presume to ask for a busy writer's time), and we sat down for lunch at her kitchen table, it was at once as if we had known each other for a long time. She wanted to hear about Norway and Scandinavia and the teaching of Canadian Studies there (she already knew a little about it from David Staines, who in 1978 had been our first Canadian guest lecturer), and she also wanted me to tell her about my book on Kate Chopin and about my wife's, Brita Lindberg-Seyersted's, study of aspects of style in Emily Dickinson's poetry. Her kind interest went further: when we sent her these books, she not only read them, but also wrote us lengthy letters about them.

Speaking about Dickinson and her language, she made a comment on the use of certain words from her own childhood:

> In a way this is an irrelevant digression, but I was [. . .] amused to learn that Emily Dickinson had used the American word "porch" and not the British "verandah", not surprisingly, but the qualitative judgements made on many words certainly do indicate a lot about particular aspects of any given society. . . . in this way words are political, of course, even when we don't realize it. I was reminded . . . and this had never actually struck me consciously before . . . that when I was a child, the word "porch" was used for the back entrance to a house, and "veranda" (that was how we spelled it) for the front entrance! One could, however, speak of both a "front" and a "back" porch, but I never heard anyone call it a "back veranda"! This must surely say something about the colonial attitudes still prevalent in the Canada of my childhood!

Her comments on my book on Chopin and the way that writer had been criticized and ostracized for her novel *The Awakening* indicate how deeply she herself had been hurt in a similar situation:

> More than anything, what moved me was the story of the reception her novel *The Awakening* received. I read that portion with *rage* at the stupidity of the reviewers and members of the reading public!! As perhaps you know (I'm sure I told you), my novel *The Diviners* was under attack here some years ago, and it was highly unpleasant and indeed awful for me. The novel was ultimately restored to the Grade 13 high school course, but it is still banned in some other parts of Canada, in high schools. I can hardly express my sense of enormous hurt and injustice and anger at that whole thing. Some

> terrible things were said about me, both in newspaper letters and in reports of open meetings at the County School Board. One I will always remember . . . one man said, in presenting a brief that called my novel obscene, blasphemous and pornographic (!), "I speak for a delegation of seven . . . myself, my wife, our four children, and God." I thought . . . there's a man who has never heard of the sin of spiritual pride! Bad enough he should presume to speak for his wife and children, but . . . for the Creator??! Well, anyway, you can see why I felt such great sympathy for Kate Chopin, being savaged, in her time, in much the same way.

In 1985, after my wife and I had sat again at Margaret Laurence's lunch table and spoken about Scandinavia, I sent her a book about Norway and an anthology (in English) of Norwegian women writers. At the same time, I invited her to come and speak at the Conference that our Nordic Association for Canadian Studies was going to have in Sweden in August, 1987. She answered that she had "promised to go to England in May 1987, for the re-issue of two of my books"; that she "just could not face making the trip to Europe twice within a few months," and that she was "so determined to finish this memoir I'm working on." But then she added:

> I wonder [. . .] if it would be at all possible for me to visit you and Brita when I am in Britain in the Spring of 1987? If this would be difficult, please don't consider it. But I would love to see a little of your beautiful country—I have long felt that there is some kind of bond between Canadians and Norwegians, possibly because of the terrain—the pictures you sent remind me a lot of northern British Columbia. Anyway, if it would be possible, I would love to do that, and perhaps meet with [. . .] some students, or whatever.

And then there was this postscript: "I am just now reading the short stories by Norwegian women—again, I sense some real spiritual-geographical connection; I feel I can hear what they are saying."

We quickly agreed that she should come to Oslo directly after the launching of the books, be shown something of the fjord country, and then, together with David Staines, take part in "The Third Hovda Seminar: An Introduction to Canada and to the Work of Margaret Laurence." (Hovda is a mountain farm, in the *Peer Gynt* and *Kristin Lavransdatter* country of central southern Norway.) The seminar was intended for professors at our teachers' training colleges, who were to read *The Stone Angel* and other writings in advance.

After several months of silence, Margaret Laurence sent a long letter dated August 1, 1986: she had been "working full out (apart from back problems, etc.)," she writes, "on these selected memoirs of mine, and I did meet my own deadline. I finished the first draft one week before my 60th birthday!" She reports on how her family and her friends had made that a truly memorable day for her, and she also speaks of the upcoming trip to England and Norway. As for the seminar, she writes that "I am not in the very least concerned with an honorarium . . . in fact, I don't want one; it will be such a great pleasure to see [. . .] something of Norway."

Only five weeks later, after she had spent a fortnight in the hospital, did the doctors give her the bad news. It is a striking illustration of her kindness and her concern for others that she at once, even before she left the hospital, should think of the practical concerns connected with the Hovda Seminar and write the following letter:

> I am afraid my trip to Norway will not now take place. I have been in hospital two weeks, and discover that I have cancer of kidney and lung, too advanced for curative treatment. Prognosis is 6 months, although of course they don't really know, one way or another. I don't feel too badly as yet. My adult children and my friends have been wonderfully supportive. I go home tomorrow, and we shall see. However, I did complete the

> first draft of my memoirs, and have made a start at typing them out—set up a mini-office in hospital! I am determined to get the second draft done, after which, if it proves necessary, my daughter (who is an editor) can edit the manuscript into submittable form. I have low moments, I need hardly to say, but I am very fortunate that my children are grown, and wonderful; that I have lived to do my lifework; and that I now have this manuscript that I hope and am determined to get into second draft . . . a goal makes a lot of difference at this point.
>
> I am so sorry I won't see Norway. [. . .] Please write from time to time . . . I'll answer if I can; if not, you'll know I am keeping my energy for this manuscript.

We did write her, and she wrote back (the last card was mailed three days before she died). She was clearly happy that David Staines and I were going through with the Hovda Seminar. We told her we would show "Margaret Laurence: The First Lady of Manawaka," the marvelous NFB film on her. In my view, no introduction to Canadian Studies could be better than the combination of that film and *The Stone Angel*, and the Hovda participants, who knew next to nothing about Canada when they came, all turned into fervent Canadianists. Equally strongly, they became adherents of Margaret Laurence. What made the meeting with her in the film and the book particularly moving to us all was of course that we knew she had intended to come. And furthermore, there were visible proofs that she had wanted to be with us in spirit. We had a sheet of paper I had sent her (where I had written, for each member of the group: "To . . ., participant in The Third Hovda Seminar"), with 20 signatures from her hand; in this way the participants could glue into their copies of *The Stone Angel* the autograph they had looked forward to asking her to give them. And she had sent us this letter, dated November 18, 1986:

[. . .] This is a difficult time, but how fortunate I am. I have two wonderful adult children, and I love their mates as well. I have lived to do my work that was given to me to do. My son (photographer) and his wife (an artist) have moved to Canada from San Francisco, to be here with me and also to establish their work in Toronto. My daughter (an excellent editor) will be married in a week's time, to a man who is a painter and also art-critic, a man who I can with no doubt say is worthy of her! My daughter-in-law has been taking care of me when David has to be in Toronto—how lucky can a person get?! My friends are so supportive and caring. In this period of my life, I sometimes feel regretful that I won't have more time, and I *hate* the "passage", even though I am deeply a Christian, albeit an unorthodox one. I don't believe in an individual immortality, but I do believe in the Holy Spirit. This has been shown to me over and over again in the last months. I feel sometimes overwhelmed by love. In this terrifying world, I still feel that there is hope.

Love,
Margaret

If you want to read this letter aloud at the Seminar, I would be honoured. If not, that's okay, too!

Photo: W.C. Christie

Kristjana Gunnars is a poet, fiction writer, critic, editor and translator. She is the author of *Settlement Poems 1 & 2*, *Wake-Pick Poems*, *The Axe's Edge* and *Night Workers of Ragnorok*. Her most recent publication is *Stephan G. Stephansson: Selected Prose & Poetry*. She is currently co-editing a collection of contemporary fiction by Icelandic-Canadian writers and writers from Iceland. She now lives in Regina.